# THE SIMPLE ARMOUR

# THE SIMPLE ARMOUR

**Maisie Wallace Gee**

Maisie Wallace Gee

ARTHUR H. STOCKWELL LTD.
Elms Court Ilfracombe Devon
*Established 1898*
*www.ahstockwell.co.uk*

*First published in Great Britain, 2007*


*British Library Cataloguing-in-Publication Data.*
*A catalogue record for this book is available from the British Library.*

*Arthur H. Stockwell Ltd. bears no responsibility for the accuracy of events recorded in this book.*

ISBN 978-0-7223-3820-9
*Printed in Great Britain by*
*Arthur H. Stockwell Ltd.*
*Torrs Park Ilfracombe*
*Devon*

'There are junctures in the affairs of men when what is wanted is a Man – not treasures, not fleets, not legions, but a Man – the man of the moment, the man of the occasion, the man of Destiny, whose spirit attracts and unites and inspires, whose capacity is congenial to the crisis, whose powers are equal to the convulsion – the child and the outcome of the storm . . . We recognise in Wallace one of these men – a man of Fate given to Scotland in the storms of the thirteenth century. It is this fact, the fact of his destiny and his fatefulness, that succeeding generations have instinctively recognised.'

*Address by Lord Rosebery, Stirling, 1897*
See Murison p. 158

# Introduction

Any account of the life and times of Sir William Wallace, the thirteenth-century Scottish patriot, must of necessity be a repetition of others. This one makes no claim to scholarship or original research; it draws heavily on the authoritative works.

From a few extant documents and fragments of evidence, historians sketch an outline of the man who burst upon the stage of Scotland's history in 1297. For all that is known of his earlier years, and indeed for a great deal of his career, we are dependent on the poem by Blind Harry, Henry the Minstrel, composed more than a century and a half after Wallace's death. If some of it is considered fabulous, there is much that can be substantiated. These fillings of tradition, presented here without apology, serve to deepen an impression it is possible to form historically without them. The diligence of biographers in their attempts to reconcile the one with the other is most gratefully acknowledged, as are the translations of the metrical chronicles to a more modernised form.

The story is a grim one, littered with probabilities and conjectures, with unreliable dates and discrepancies. 'The writer must resign himself' wrote Professor Murison in 1898 'to the simple if somewhat perilous course of telling his story as it has shaped itself in his mind during perusal of the available authorities.' Nowadays, with 'histories' blossoming in some profusion, age-old traditions that have some basis in fact are brushed aside or distorted by changing fashions in construction and interpretation.

But of this much there is no doubt: the youthful Wallace rebelled against oppression; he gave his manhood to the fight for freedom and the independence of his country; he gave his life for the liberty of the common people, who for generations after were sustained and inspired by his example. He is sometimes dismissed as unimportant in that his nine-year struggle against Edward I of England did not change the course of history, and on this point the reader will form a judgement.

Opinion is usually extreme; Wallace is regarded either as a noble champion of his country's cause, or branded a cold-blooded barbarian. This brief narrative seeks only to redress the balance, to throw light on a great historic figure about whom – in the southern part of the United Kingdom at least – little is known.

The Age of Chivalry and Crusade was a time of horrific cruelty also, and it is against this background that events must be considered. To his countrymen William Wallace may need no recommendation, to others no defence, except against injustice and a theory that it is to his death and martyrdom – rather than to his life – that he owes his position as the National Hero of Scotland.

The family estate in his time and long after was called Ellerslie and this is used in preference to the later spelling, Elderslie (which probably came about due to a spelling error). There is confusion still over some of the leading personalities involved; the brief genealogy tables, provided solely for the assistance of the reader, are as accurate as limited research will allow.

Out of several 'histories of Scotland' the relevant volumes of George Buchanan and John Hill Burton have the greater appeal, perversely perhaps, because the former, acknowledged as one of the most learned men of his day (1505–1582), is criticised, discredited even, for being too partisan. Burton (1809–1881), Historiographer Royal for Scotland, is for some unimaginative!

# Acknowledgements

Acknowledgements are due to the Council and secretary of the Scottish Text Society for the extracts from Moir's edition of *Wallace*; to Adam Fergusson for passages from his late father's book, *William Wallace*; to A. M. Heath & Co. Ltd. for the extract from McLaren's *If Freedom Fail*; to the editor of the *Glasgow Evening Times* for the lines from Brotchie's *Sylvan Scenes*; to the Directors of Burke's *Peerage* Ltd. for some details in the genealogy tables; to D. J. W. Pryce, Department of the Environment, for the information on the brass tablet on the steps in Westminster Hall; to HMSO for permission to use the illustration of Mrs Frances Dunlop in *Robert Burns, Pride and Passion* by Gavin Sprott, 1996; to all who took time and trouble to answer my letters and queries; and to my family, especially to my brother-in-law Robert Freestone for his guidance.

That wonderful institution the second-hand bookshop has proved invaluable; and lastly I thank the staff of Devizes Region Branch of Wiltshire Public Library for their help and interest, 1978.

Further acknowledgements are due to Vanecia Halpin, Judy Head, and to my nephew Colin Naman my undying gratitude for producing the final computerised copy, and to them all for the giving of their time.

*M.W.G., 2003*

# Chapter I

Not since William did this England 'lie at the proud foot of a conqueror'. It is therefore difficult sometimes to understand the spirit of nationalism that prevails in the so-called Celtic areas of these islands.

To appreciate any one part of a picture it is necessary to unroll the canvas. About 600 BC, so the ethnologists tell us, Celtic races migrating from Europe invaded Albion, land of the white cliffs, unknown then to be the largest of a group of islands. In three separate waves they came, some two hundred years between each immigration, all of the same basic stock though of differing build and colouring. These were the 'Ancient Britons' that the Roman general Julius Caesar encountered when he landed in Kent in August 55 BC to carry out a survey. In AD 41 the conquest began in earnest, and, driven to the northern and western parts of the country, and to the neighbouring island of Hibernia (Ireland), the Celts established their kingdoms. When the Romans finally left Britain in AD 410, the fierce unconquered tribes swarmed over the Great Wall built by the Emperor Hadrian to contain them, to terrorise the now defenceless Romanised population.

In the next two centuries Britain was invaded by the Teutonic races – Jutes, Saxons and Angles – and in the ninth century by the Danes. The Britons again retreated to the mountainous regions of the north and west, maintaining their kingdoms of Strathclyde and Cumbria, Wales and West Wales (Cornwall). The newcomers founded colonies which in time became separate kingdoms. As the larger swallowed up the smaller the land of the Angles became known as England, and a new race evolved.

The last king of the Anglo-Saxon line was Edward the Confessor, later St Edward. Foreign in upbringing, language and customs, he left the running of the country to Godwin, Earl of Wessex. On his deathbed Edward named as his successor Godwin's son, the just and able Earl Harold, for a decade the actual ruler of England and hastily crowned Harold II on 5 January 1066. Across the Channel, William Duke of Normandy, Edward's cousin, made claim to England by descent and by promise, and with the blessing of the Pope prepared to invade. He landed at Pevensey, Sussex, on 28 September 1066, killing Harold and winning the Battle of Hastings.

Under the masterly rule of William I, England became one kingdom. The Norman Conquest, though it brought order and cultural advancement, engendered in the breast of the 'native' population a hatred and envy of the Norman barons and adventurers, who between them in the twenty-one years of the Conqueror's reign acquired as their personal possessions almost all the shires of England. Great mansions, churches and castles they built to defend and maintain their 'rights'.

Heir by descent was the grandson of Edmund Ironside, Edgar the Atheling; on the death of Harold, Edgar was chosen King of England by the Witan – the Council of Wise Men – but the boy was never crowned. With his sister he took refuge from the Normans at the court of the Scottish king, Malcolm III, who married the pious Margaret. The Conqueror's fourth and youngest son, married to Edith[1] only daughter of Malcolm and Margaret, claimed the crown of England in 1100, as Henry I. These two marriages united ancient royal lines, making popular and fashionable the fusion of the races.

On 13 July 1174 a party of English barons captured William the Lion, King of Scotland on English soil and carried him to their king at Northampton. William was removed to Normandy and under the Treaty of Falaise gained his freedom by admitting Henry II of England to be Lord Superior of Scotland, and rendering to him complete homage. Henry was succeeded by his third son, Richard I, Coeur de Lion, then aged thirty-two. Immediately after his coronation at Westminster in 1189 Richard prepared for the Third Crusade, to free the Holy Land from the Saracen leader Saladin. To pay for the expedition the King sold everything he could lay hands on. Lands belonging to Crown and Church, even offices of state, were sold to the highest bidders. William paid over to Richard 10,000 marks; English suzerainty was cancelled and Scottish independence restored.

Alexander III came to the throne on 7 July 1249, supported by a regency since he was barely eight years old. Six days later, seated on the Stone of Destiny at Scone, he was crowned King of Scotland. The grandson of William the Lion, in 1251 he married Margaret, the eleven-year-old daughter of Henry III of England. Pressures brought to bear on the boy encouraged the growth of nationalism. The atmosphere was such that when Henry invited Alexander and his wife to visit London the regents insisted on a solemn assurance that the young king would not be involved in any treaties, and that should Margaret's baby be born there it would not be detained. A daughter was born in 1260; two sons followed and in 1275 the Queen died. Ten years later Alexander married Joleta, daughter of the Count de Dreux. Aware of the machinations at the time of his own accession and minority, the King had taken steps to ensure the succession. The younger of his two sons, David, died in boyhood; Alexander, heir to the throne, grew to manhood and married a daughter of the Count of Flanders, but he too died without issue. The King's only daughter, Margaret, married Eric II of Norway. Their daughter, also Margaret, born in 1283 and known as the Maid of Norway, was acknowledged by parliament as heiress to the Scottish throne.

On the death of Henry III in 1272, his eldest son, the proud Lord Edward, ascended the throne of England. Before attending the coronation Alexander again demanded guarantees that his visit would not affect his independence. As the King of England was required to render homage to the King of France for lands and estates he held in that country, so in 1278 did Alexander formally render it to Edward for such possessions as he held in England. The English document is said to show his 'unconditional homage', the writing being over an erasure and suspected of deliberate falsification. A record of the ceremony, made by a Scots monastic scribe and preserved in Dunfermline Abbey is 'precise' and concludes 'with Alexander saying aloud "To homage for my kingdom of Scotland no one has right but God alone, nor do I hold it of any, but of God." ' And so he preserved his independence, while maintaining friendship with his ambitious brother-in-law.

Early in 1286 Alexander summoned a Council, its purpose being to arrange the release of hostages. Lords and nobles travelled to Edinburgh Castle for 18/19 March. The company was congenial, the wining and dining prolonged, and with the King in jovial mood the matter of succession would naturally and easily be mooted, the infant Maid across the water an uninspiring prospect in the unhappy event of the King's demise. What king and country desired above all was a healthy male heir, growing to maturity under the tutelage of a wise father. In good health himself and with a young wife, issue from this union could be happily anticipated. In this assembly of hearty men, replete with food and wine, reticence was unlikely. There would be ribaldry and good-natured guffaws, stimulating the King's resolve to join his wife at Kinghorn. His determination to reach her must be seen as a denial of the rumours that the Queen was already pregnant. Neither howling wind, rain and sleet or the gathering darkness deterred him, and with a small escort on foot Alexander rode down from the castle and at Queensferry was rowed across the Forth, from where, against all advice he set off again along the coast of Fife. In the black fury and noise of the storm the guides lost sight and sound of their charge, who either rode his horse over the cliff or the animal stumbled, throwing both to their death.

The untimely end of a beloved and enlightened ruler was to leave his bride a widow in a strange cold land, and plunge his distraught people from a century of peace into a long and bitter struggle.

# Chapter II

Edward I of England was on crusade at the time of his accession. Returning home two years later, aged thirty-five, he was in the very prime of manhood, a lean athletic figure. Nicknamed 'Longshanks' he stood head and shoulders above most of his contemporaries, his once yellow hair darkened, his good looks marred only by a slightly drooping left eyelid.[1] At the age of fifteen he married Eleanor, the ten-year-old daughter of Ferdinand III, and half-sister of King Alphonso of Castile. Eleanor grew into a handsome and remarkable woman whose strength of character equalled that of her husband. She accompanied him on all his travels, and the marriage was successful and happy.

Edward acquired a fearsome reputation, both in battle and on the sporting field; a man of moods and violent temper, magnanimous to those who bent to his will, without mercy to any who opposed it. Due to his father's extravagant tastes and lavish spending, the country was almost bankrupt. Henry III it was who rebuilt Westminster Abbey and in so doing practically emptied the nation's purse. His son was made of sterner stuff, and at once took an iron hold on the affairs of his realm. The joint coronation of Edward and Eleanor in the Abbey on 19 August 1274 was unprecedented in splendour and joyful celebration. Possessing an astute legal mind, the new king instituted reforms, and under the great Statutes enacted in the earlier part of his reign, the English nation took shape and stability.

His first two sons, John and Henry, died in early childhood. The third, Alphonso, heir to the throne, died at the age of eleven. By 1284 Wales had been subdued and the castles built. It was the King's fourth son, Edward, born at Caernarvon that same year, who in 1301 was created first English Prince of Wales. In the meantime, ambassadors were scurrying back and forth across the North Sea to Norway, arranging the marriage of the Prince to the Maid, now Queen of Scotland. The far-sighted English monarch had already obtained from Pope Honorius IV a bull permitting him to marry his children to relatives in 'certain degrees of affinity'. In all his negotiations, Edward, solicitous for his grand-niece, stressed the unsettled condition of Scotland. If she were placed in his care, he would, on the establishment of peace and security – and when the people demanded it – send their queen to them.

By March 1290, when Margaret was seven, all was amicably settled. The Six Guardians of Scotland addressed letters to King Edward assenting to the marriage, and to King Eric urging that she be sent to England 'free from matrimonial engagement'. But Eric was reluctant to part with his frail daughter, and the splendidly appointed vessel, fitted out at Yarmouth and sent by Edward in May, returned in June without her.

Under the Treaty of Birgham (18 July 1290), by mutual consent Scotland was to remain a free and separate kingdom, until such time as children should spring from the marriage 'who could take on them the management of the realm'. But if no children were born, or should die before maturity, 'then the kingdom of Scotland should revert to the nearest of kin in the royal line'.[2]

In the autumn Queen Margaret set sail and Edward dispatched his representative, Antony Bek, Bishop of Durham to meet her at Orkney, then a province of Norway. Costly gifts of furs and jewels befitting the bride-to-be of his son and heir were provided for her use. But the little queen was never to see her kingdom or her bridegroom; she died on the journey, either from seasickness or, as one story goes, from a surfeit of figs. News of her death came through only as rumours. 'There was' says Burton, 'none of the solemn detail that might be expected to attend a royal death. Of the place where she died and is buried nothing is known.'[3] That the child queen's body was returned to and identified by her father, and buried beside her mother at Bergen, is made 'abundantly clear from documents of Bishop Audfinn of Bergen, now in the Royal Library at Stockholm, translated from the "barbarous Dano-Norse" by Joseph Anderson, and published in Scotland in 1872'.[4] Although at the time the facts of the matter must have been known to a few – who found it advantageous to maintain secrecy – the truth did not filter through to the Scottish people as a whole, and ten years later, when Eric had been succeeded by his brother Haco, a young woman came forward claiming to be the Maid. Her story, that she had been kidnapped at Orkney by a woman of high rank whom she named, was circumstantial and secured support. Tried as an impostor and a witch, she was found guilty and sentenced to be burnt at the stake, holding to her story to the last. Had King Eric been alive in 1301 the affair might never have arisen, or the outcome been different. It is less idle to speculate, however, that but for the King of England's great personal sorrow at the time of Margaret's reported death, the web of silence and suspicion would have been satisfactorily untangled.

A letter dated 7 October 1290 reached Edward about the time that Queen Eleanor died (28 November), aged forty-six. His wife for thirty-five years, all her adult life at his side, a loving companion and, most probably, a wise counsellor, she bore him fifteen children.

In June 1272 while on crusade, Edward was stabbed with a poison dagger by an Arab of the Assassin sect, and became seriously ill. The romantic story of Eleanor saving her husband's life by sucking the poison from his wound unfortunately carried little weight. Surgery saved him, and, as Agnes Strickland points out, 'the narrators who describe the scene so minutely, would not have forgotten the circumstance'.[5] Her body was borne from Nottingham to London by the grief-stricken king, halting at principal churches en route, and at Westminster Eleanor was buried with due pomp. At all the stopping-places, in the following year the King erected memorial crosses, twelve in all, of which three remain: at Hardingstone near Northampton, at Geddington near Kettering, and at Waltham Cross, giving the place its name. The cross at the village of Charing was removed in 1614 and a copy erected in 1864.

The letter, from William Fraser, Bishop of St Andrews, brought to Edward rumours of Queen Margaret's death, urging him – should the report unhappily be true – to come to the Border and prevent bloodshed, and to assist in placing the rightful successor on the throne of Scotland. The ensuing squabbles of her nobles gave him the opportunity he needed to extend his rule, and towards that country the King of England now directed his ambition.

Of the twelve or more contenders for the throne, most were descendants of Norman nobles who came with the Conqueror, with lands and possessions in England. To have incurred Edward's displeasure would put their wealth at risk, and having no deep-rooted love for the country or its people, they were content to leave matters in his hands.

Requesting the Scots nobles to meet him on his own soil, at Norham on 10 May 1291, King Edward appeared before them in the full regalia of monarchy. His justiciar, Sir Roger le Brabazon, recited the long preamble and concluded by saying "the King doth require your hearty recognition of his rights as your superior and overlord". The 'astonished' Scots requested an adjournment; this being granted, they were instructed by the Bishop of Durham to produce what evidence they could against Edward's superiority. On 2 June, in an open field near Upsettlington, both sides had men in arms. The Chancellor of England informed the assembly that as the Scots had brought forth no evidence to disprove Edward's overlordship, the King would now proceed to investigate the rights of the claimants to the throne, all of whom were required to swear on oath that they would stand by his decree.

Robert Bruce, 5th Lord of Annandale, and Sir John Baliol were the finalists. Sir John Comyn (the Black Comyn) withdrew and gave his support to Baliol, his brother-in-law. Edward invited Bruce and Baliol to select forty auditors each, while he produced twenty-four to advise him, all these to hear the evidence of the contestants and report to him for his supreme judgement.

The six Guardians, the Earls of Fife and Buchan and the Bishop of St Andrews for the north; James the High Steward, the Bishop of Glasgow and Sir John Comyn, Lord of Badenoch for the south, on 11 June 1291 resigned the kingdom of Scotland and its castles, and 'all who would have been bound to make homage to a living king of Scotland' were ordered to swear it to Edward. Among those who failed to render homage, and who never did so, was a lesser knight from Ellerslie, Sir Malcolm Wallace.

The population generally were not immediately aware of their subjugation; it was brought home to them by the imposition of English laws and customs; by the replacement of Scots by Englishmen in all high positions and offices of state. Edward installed deputies in the towns, through whom the barons and lords could render their homage, and from this time Scotland was virtually an occupied country.

In the long drawn-out legal proceedings the eighty auditors had no voice, and a petition from the Community[6] that he should act only as arbitrator the King studiously ignored. His own auditors he shut in a church, no one to have access to them, though from time to time he went in alone, 'and by discoursing with them separately he found the majority of opinion, that the preferable right belonged to Baliol'.[7] The documents were sealed in a sack and deposited in Berwick Castle. The cause dragged on until 17 November 1292 when, with an impressive display of legality and amid much grandeur, Edward decreed John Baliol the lawful successor. A few days later the malleable John rendered homage to Edward, and that king broke the Great Seal of Scotland into four pieces. On payment of twenty pounds John received his kingdom and was crowned at Scone on 30 November. 'According to the law as now established' writes Burton, 'it was a correct judgement, and probably the full consideration which the case received may have done much to settle the rule of primogeniture for aftertimes.'[8]

Under Alexander III the Scots enjoyed what was for the times an orderly society, the laws which he enacted seeming fair and just to all sections of the community. He divided the country into four, spending three months in each quarter. The sheriff of the district would meet him on arrival and escort him at his departure to the boundaries of jurisdiction, where the same procedure operated. By this means the King knew his people and became known to them, rich and poor alike having access to him. Thirteenth-century Scotland presented a peaceful and prosperous face, engaging in flourishing trade with neighbouring countries. It was a golden age. This way of life the spirited people were determined to hold on to; they neither wanted nor expected alien domination, and the overthrow of their nationhood by a few disinterested nobles was to be resisted by any means.

From the beginning John was a puppet king and the country seethed with unrest. For often trivial reasons he was repeatedly summoned to London to give account of himself, and treated to studied humiliations in the courts. In like manner Philip IV of France summoned Edward as his vassal, to answer for serious disputes in the Channel between marauding seamen from both sides, with heavy losses to the French in ships and crews. But Edward did not himself go to France, and the covetous Philip used the episode as a means of annexing the properties of Gascony and Aquitaine. Edward prepared for war, promising the citizens of Guienne that he would shortly free them 'from a yoke they abhorred'.

The immediate necessity in mastering the kingdoms adjoining his own was to provide Edward with unlimited supplies of manpower for his dispute with France. Wales was again in revolt, and the army intended for embarkation had first to put down hostilities there. As overlord of Scotland he demanded that King John raise an army and join forces in London by September 1294. John attended, but his barons ignored the summons. In 1295 they called a parliament, dismissing all English court officials and appointing twelve of their own.

Whatever his weaknesses, John was placed in an intolerable position, and in that year, perhaps in desperation, signed a treaty of mutual aid with Philip. Edward got wind of this 'treachery' and in a document dated 16 October he engaged 'his beloved and faithful John' to deliver over three frontier castles. The Scots refused the conditions.

In November Edward called to his famous Model Parliament representatives from every shire and borough. Baliol was required to expel all French and Flemish merchants; lands held in England by the Scots king and others were confiscated, and all goods on such lands sold. Fighting broke out in Berwick and some English merchants were killed. Baliol was summoned to Newcastle to account for the trouble, but, roused at last to resistance, failed to appear – or was prevented by his barons. "The felon fool" stormed Edward, "if he will not come to us, we will go to him." An army of 30,000 foot and 5,000 horse – which nothing was allowed to hinder – marched to Wark, on the Borders.

On 26 March 1296 the Earl of Buchan led a large party of Scots into Cumberland and Northumberland, wasting and burning the monasteries of Hexham and Lanercost. As Murison remarks, 'these futile and inglorious efforts of retaliation' contributed nothing to the cause; Buchan's troops returned home and installed themselves in Dunbar Castle. On 28 March the English army crossed the Tweed at Coldstream, and two days later there followed what has been described as 'the most disastrous crime in British history'.[9] So rich and prosperous was the city of Berwick that its taxable value was equal to the rest of the country put together; it was the centre of trade and culture, and one of the most important seaports in the British Isles. On Edward's orders and in his presence the city was sacked, its citizens massacred, 7,000 the lowest estimate slain. No man, woman or child was spared and the streets were said to be 'rivers of blood'.[10] All day long the slaughter continued until Edward witnessed an incident to turn even his hardened stomach, and called off his troops. Given the events of that day, reports of his distress over the sight of a child clinging to its mother tend to stretch credulity; less palatable but nearer the truth is the chronicler Wyntoun's version, of an unborn child bursting from the side of a murdered woman:

'This kyng Edward saw in that tyde
A woman slain, and of her syde
A bairn he saw fall out sprewland,
Beside that woman slain lyand;'[11]

Some French and Flemish merchants still remained and held out in their own Red Hall. All perished when the building was fired by the invaders. Thus did the King of England himself set the pattern for violence and terror that was to imprint itself on the very heart of Scotland. By wrecking the port of Berwick he scored on both fronts, destroying not only Scotland's trade, but damaging that of France. The castle, commanded by Sir William Douglas, surrendered the same day, the lives of its garrison guaranteed on taking oaths of allegiance to Edward.

In April, after a furious battle Dunbar Castle fell to John de Warenne, Earl of Surrey. A few nobles and a great number of knights, 'the flower of Scotland's fighting strength', fell into enemy hands, to be imprisoned in English strongholds. Edward's armies continued northward, plundering and destroying as they went, teaching a lesson to all who would oppose their overlord. In the abbey at Scone were housed the symbols of monarchy; a previous relic, the Black Rood, a 'certified fragment' of the Cross of Christ, brought to Scotland by the sainted Queen Margaret, had special significance for the people. The Stone of Destiny, believed to have been Jacob's Pillow and taken to Scotland by Scotia, daughter of Pharaoh, was perhaps the most honoured possession because of the prophecy associated with it:

'Where'er is found this sacred Stone
The Scottish race shall reign.'

All these treasures Edward removed. The Stone, on which all Scottish kings were seated for their crowning, he enshrined in a specially built Coronation Chair at Westminster. There, regardless of arguments about its authenticity, it has remained ever since, except for a brief absence when on Christmas Day 1950 it was spirited away from the Abbey by Scottish Nationalists, but was recovered and used at the Coronation of Elizabeth II on 2 June 1953.

Edward progressed in triumph through the country, meeting little resistance. On 7 July 1296 in the churchyard of Stracathro, King John on his knees rendered penance to Antony Bek, Bishop of Durham, and there surrendered his robes. Three days later at Brechin Castle, he resigned his throne, lands and goods. Baliol, a lover of fine clothes, was nicknamed 'Toom Tabard' (empty coat) by his subjects. Giving his only son Edward as his pledge, he was secretly conveyed to England by sea, and at Hertford allowed to live the life of a country gentleman, within a twenty-mile radius. He was forty-seven. The provision of a house, suite and pension for the deposed king seems less of a kindly gesture when it is remembered that the Scottish Treasury and revenue from the confiscated estates of Baliol and his barons was now in Edward's hands.

In August he called a parliament at Berwick to receive submission from the nobles and their subordinates, signatories to the Ragman Rolls.[12] Baliol's wife Isobel was the youngest daughter of the Earl of Surrey, who was appointed by the King Governor of Scotland. A churchman, Sir Hugh de Cressingham, was to be treasurer; Sir William de Ormsby, justiciar. Sir Henry de Percy, knighted by the King at the onset of the campaign in March, was appointed Warden of Galloway and Ayr, and Castellan of Ayr, Wigton, Cruggleton, and Buittle, on 8 September 1296, a heavy responsibility for a young man of about twenty-four. Arrangements for governing the country complete, the King proclaimed his peace throughout the realm, and remarking to one of his courtiers "a man does well who rids himself of dirt," took off for London.

Much devastation and loss of life could have been avoided had the native population of Scotland passively accepted foreign domination; kings were impatient men, and a gradual progression was not in Edward's scheme of things. He left behind him a team of ruthless greedy men, and a rapacious soldiery. Insurrections were soon breaking out, at first on a local scale. The rebellious people, driven to defend themselves against their oppressors, waged guerilla-type warfare however and whenever they could. The removal of their lords and clergy from high office, and the confiscation of records and documents, they took as an affront to their race and lineage. They could not have known – or thought it their business if they had – that the seeds of democratic government, sown by Simon de Montfort[12] in his parliament on 28 January 1265, had taken root in the fertile mind of Edward I of England.

In the light of twentieth-century history, to blame the Scots for the ills that beset their land in the thirteenth is surely irrational. Unlike the brave men and women of Occupied Europe in the Second World War (1939–1945), whose patriotism paved the way for the Allied landings in Normandy on 6 June 1944, the Scots in 1296 had neither direction or encouragement, nor assistance from any quarter. But then, as in 1940, a tall man was emerging from obscurity.

# Chapter III

All documents from monasteries and religious houses King Edward ordered to be searched for proof of his overlordship, but nothing conclusive was found. While it may not have been his intention at the time permanently to remove these records, in the course of events they were for ever lost. John of Fordun, a priest in the diocese of St Andrews, and chaplain of the church of Aberdeen, lived during the reigns of Robert II (1371–1390) and III (1390–1406). He has been styled 'the father of Scottish history', searching the private records and libraries of the country, and those of England and Ireland likewise, piecing together the history of the nation from its origins to the time of David I (1153). Fordun's continuator was Walter Bower, Abbot of Inchcolm, and it is he who writes of William Wallace in the work commonly referred to as Fordun's. This chronicle, known as the *Scotichronicon* and continued by others to the death of James I (1437), 'is the oldest and most respected authority'.[1]

Another reliable recorder is Andrew of Wyntoun, Prior of the Monastery of St Serf. His *Orygynale Cronykil of Scotland*, completed about 1426, is a further source of information about Wallace, whose school companion at Dundee, John Blair, later to be his chaplain, became a Benedictine monk and wrote in Latin prose an account of the Patriot's life. A contemporary English chronicler, Walter of Hemingburgh[2] is regarded as an authentic reporter and is widely quoted.

The only existing 'authority' on Wallace's early years is the poem by Henry the Minstrel (Blind Harry),[3] which he professes to base on the account by Blair and his associate, Thomas Gray, a parson of Liberton. The work has been derided as 'romantic nonsense', dismissed altogether by some historians, given some credibility by others. Nevertheless it stands, a monument to its author's hero, and no less to the Minstrel himself. Lord Hailes, examining the poem in his *Annals of Scotland*, 1776, was mainly responsible for its being discredited as historic fact. But since that time documents have come to light confirming Harry in some of the disputed passages of his narrative. Mr Joseph Stevenson of Durham, when a sub-commissioner of Public Records, made important discoveries in the Tower of London. Although the Minstrel's writings have no place in the *Wallace Papers*, which he edits, and in spite of 'serious errors and exaggerations', Mr Stevenson has this to say of the poem: 'the present collection of documents places this subject in a new and interesting position, for it shows that the particulars . . . are in reality genuine and authentic history'.[4] His protest at the 'sweeping condemnation' of the Minstrel is emphasised by Professor Murison in his Preface; and 'without his aid' says Paterson, 'no *life* of Wallace can be written'. It is of course important to keep the traditional chronicles in the right perspective, and here the historian John Hill Burton is of the greatest assistance:

'What it is of moment to remember is that, during several centuries when Scotland had no recorder of passing events, England had always one or more, contemporary with the times of which he was the annalist . . . Scotland must take the account of her conduct almost entirely from the side of the enemy. When Scotsmen began to write their own annals they did so in a tone of vehement patriotism, inspired by the hot struggle not yet over. Barbour's *Bruce* was written about 1350, Blind Harry's *Wallace* a century later . . . It may be questioned if either author reaches the standard of poetry according to the aesthetic notions of the present day, nor indeed, did their task as rhyming chroniclers demand that they should. Andrew of Wyntoun . . . is less poetic than the others, and his idea of his task would probably have rendered him as grateful for compliments to his poetic power as any historian of later times is to those who call him flowery or imaginative. To many of the metrical chroniclers, indeed, the use of rhyme rather served for restraining verbal luxuriance than for encouraging poetic licence. The couplet became the measure within which a distinctive assertion or proposition had to be set forth.'[5]

Though no positive date emerges from any of these writings, the generally accepted time of Wallace's birth is 1270–1274, at Ellerslie, to the west of Paisley in Renfrewshire. The popular image is of a peasant, working on his father's estate and brooding over the fate of his country, rising suddenly in 1297 to lead a rabble army against the

English. Certainly his achievements would seem the more remarkable if this were so, but the picture is inaccurate. His forbears, most likely of the old Celtic stock from the ancient kingdom of Strathclyde, then bordering Wales, can be traced to the reign of David I. Sir James Fergusson provides a neat assessment: 'a large and ancient class of profound though unostentatious influence . . . Wallace's blood carried with it the tradition of authority and leadership, of long attachment to the Scottish soil, and of hereditary service to the royal house.'[6]

David I, third son of Malcolm III and (Saint) Margaret, was brought up in England, and from 1108 held the Earldom of Huntingdon. Coming to the throne of Scotland in 1124 he appointed as his High Steward one Walter Fitz Alan,[7] the learned son of a Shropshire baron of Norman descent. Walter founded Paisley Abbey and Richard Walense – or Waleys – witnessed the charters in 1173. He acquired extensive estates, naming the place where he settled Riccard-toun. Three generations later comes Sir Malcolm Wallace, who at the time of his marriage, so Harry tells us:

'Ellerslie then had in heritage
Auchinbothie, and other sundrie place.
The great-grandson he was of good Wallace.'
*[Book I, lines 28–30]*

Malcolm's wife Margaret came of an equally ancient and respected family, of Anglo-Danish origin. Early in the thirteenth century a Sir Reginald (Ranald) Craufurd was created hereditary Sheriff of Ayr, and married the heiress of Loudoun. It was his grandson of whom it was said:

'So in his time he had a daughter fair;
And young Sir Ranald sheriff of that town,
His sister fair, of good fame and renown;
Malcolm Wallace her got in marriage.'
*[Book I, lines 24–27]*

William was the second son; a Sir John Wallace, executed in London in 1307, may have been a third. Nothing is known of him save this fact, but since he was knighted and suffered the same fate, he undoubtedly gave himself to the cause. Indeed, the actions of all three may have been attributed to the one, as the Marquess of Bute

points out. We learn too of two sisters who must have been much older – probably from an earlier marriage of Sir Malcolm's – as their sons, Edward Little and Tom Halliday were among William's earliest supporters.

From the death of Alexander III, the Wallaces of Ellerslie suffered a setback in their fortunes – a point not always taken into account. The marriage of Alexander II and Joan, sister of Henry III of England, was childless, and there was no heir to the throne. To remedy this the King publicly named as his successor Robert Bruce, 5th Lord of Annandale. But late in his reign the King's second wife presented him with a son, pushing Bruce out of the running. Following the accidental death of this third Alexander, Bruce, ignoring the child queen Margaret, headed a conspiracy for power against the Baliol-Comyn faction, and for two years hostilities raged between them, amounting almost to civil war. The Brucian party pledged themselves to the Lord Richard de Burgh, Earl of Ulster and King Edward's close friend. They sent to the six regents a threatening letter that 'in certain circumstances' they would have recourse to the King of England; James, 5th High Steward, and his brother John were among the fourteen nobles who signed, on 20 September 1286, what is known as the Turnbury Bond. The Wallaces, vassals of the Steward, 'failed to follow the line taken by their superior, and in consequence of their opposition to the political principles, or rather the want of principles of their Lord . . .' the family home at Ellerslie was broken up. Forced eventually to leave, Sir Malcolm retired to the Lennox, in Dumbartonshire, taking with him his eldest son Malcolm, first placing his wife and second son in the care of her father's uncle, an aged priest living at Kilspindie in the Carse of Gowrie. Here it was thought William could continue his education.

Almost certainly schooled by the monks at the Abbey of Paisley, he had in all probability been prepared for a life of dedication to the Church. From childhood his tutors kindled in his mind a passion for freedom and liberty. Add to this the patriotic ardour instilled and nourished by the Priest of Dunipace, said to be his father's brother, and it will hardly be surprising that he set himself to the pursuit of these two inestimable blessings with all the fervour of headstrong youth. This priest is not found in the genealogy, where his father is said to have but one brother. Known as William's uncle, he could well have been his father's. Harry describes him as 'a man of great riches, a mighty person, called to name Wallas'.

It was while they were at Kilspindie, probably, that William and his mother learned of the death of Sir Malcolm, slain at Loudoun Hill in combat with the English. His eldest son is said to have died in the same battle, but this is doubted for at least two reasons. Wyntoun, referring to William's position in 1297 says:

'Hys eldare brodyre the herytage
Had, and joyfyd in hys dayis.'

And this brother is on the scene two years hence, as we shall see.

At his approaching manhood, William must already have been a personable specimen, of impressive physique. 'His mental culture' says the Marquess of Bute, 'would be that of a person in the corresponding position today. Sir William Wallace at least knew how to read and write in three language – his own, Latin and French – and it seems he also knew Gaelic. He knew the ancient and modern history, and the common mathematics and science of his own day.' The family would be, according to the Marquess, 'unpretentious country gentry in a position of easy fortune, attached by tradition and politics, and probably by feudal dependence, to the great house of the High Steward of Scotland. There would be a surrounding of peasants working at Ellerslie, receiving no wages, and tenants feudally attached.'[8] This is the background of the youth whose path we are to follow.

With the surrender of the castles to Edward in 1291, English soldiers took over the garrison towns, treating the population as a conquered people, and William was 'right oft in strife'. Man's attitude to man having changed but little since those days, we can, nearly seven hundred years later, understand his growing resentment at the oppression of his family, the brutality and violence practised against his countrymen, and the day-to-day insults of an insolent invader.

'Sad of countenance, he was both old and young:
Little of speech, wise, courteous and benign.'
*[Book I, lines 201–202]*

He was eighteen years old when, according to Harry, with four companions he strolled into the sporting place at Dundee. It was perhaps the spring of 1292. Dressed in green with a plaid mantle, a knife in his belt and sword at his side, he was at once assailed by a youth named Selby, son of the English governor of the castle[9], who took him to task for being so attired. William withstood the taunts and restrained himself until Selby tried to wrest his knife, and for this gross insult struck him dead on the spot. In normal circumstances, at a time when men lived by the sword – and certainly had the situation been reversed – this action would have been considered one of honour. In the existing ones it was the first serious mark against the young Scot, and he was outlawed by the English. He eluded his pursuers by sheltering in the house of a crofter known to his father. The wife, who was busily spinning, enveloped him in a robe and set him to work. By the time the searchers opened the door he was covered in fluff, and they failed to recognise the industrious spinner. William was entertained by his protectors, the grain-knocker on which he sat being preserved by their descendants.[10] Disguised as pilgrims, he and his mother left Kilspindie for Dunipace, where they were invited to stay, but they declined, and made their way to Ellerslie. Lady Wallace was anxious for the annulment of the outlawry. Since this necessitated submission to King Edward, William scornfully rejected any such relief, following the example of his father, and the doctrine of his uncle, the Priest of Dunipace:

"My son, I tell thee soothfastlie,
No gift is like to Libertie;
Then never live in slaverie."

His resolve to drive out or destroy the enemy wherever he found him was undoubtedly strengthened from this time, and, to keep him from further trouble and danger, William was sent to his paternal uncle, Sir Richard Wallace, the Lord of Riccarton.

On the 'three and twenty day of April' he was fishing in the Irvine. 'Lord Percy' and his train passed by on their way to Glasgow Fair. Five English soldiers hung back, demanding William's abundant catch, supposedly for a religious festival. He amicably handed over some of the fish, protesting mildly at further demands because, he said, "it was for an aged knight". One soldier drew a sword and rushed upon the Scot, who felled him with the fishing pole, seized the sword and slew his opponent. The other four set upon him and two more he killed, the remaining two fleeing after the train to enlist support. Their tale of five armed troops against one unarmed fisherman Percy treated with scorn and no help was forthcoming. William could not now remain at Riccarton and expose his blind and elderly uncle to the expected repercussions of his act. Taking leave of Sir Richard, who furnished him with money and necessities and the promise of more, he rode off to Laglane Woods with the horses of his assailants, refusing to allow his cousins to accompany him.

Soon tired of inactivity, he ventured one day into Ayr, leaving his horse with his 'child' at the edge of the wood, 'as then na man had he' – this remark of Harry's is in itself an implication of Wallace's youth, that he was attended only by a child. In the town a champion of huge dimensions boasted his superiority over the Scots, in the manner of the times. For a groat he invited all comers to strike his back with a rod. Eager for the sport William offered three groats, and landed a blow that broke the boaster's back. He was at once attacked by the English, five of whom he killed in his escape to the woods.

At Ayr the sheriff's servant was buying fish in the marketplace. Percy sent his steward on the same errand and this man insultingly demanded the first one's purchases. Arriving on the scene and making 'gentle remonstrance' William was struck with a hunting staff. He grabbed the steward by the collar and stabbed him to the heart. Eighty soldiers were on duty keeping order in the marketplace, and set upon him. Drawing his sword he charged into the throng and cut down several more, until himself brought to the ground. Orders were that he should not be killed, but left to pine, a prisoner in the old gaol at Ayr.[11] The laments of his womenfolk, their pleas for his tender age, moved his gaolers not at all:

'His kyn might not him get for no kind thing,
Might they have paid the ransom of a king.
The more they bid, the more it was in vain;
Of their best men that day seven he had slain.'
*[Book I, lines 149–152]*

Lying wounded in a foul cell and fed on only salted herring and water, he became very ill. How long he was left to 'pine' we are not to know. A gaoler sent to bring him up for judgement found him seemingly lifeless from 'the flux', and reported that the prisoner had 'payed highly for his misdeeds'. Without further advice the 'corpse' was thrown over the prison wall onto a dung-heap. An old family nurse hearing of his fate went to see for herself, and on her knees requested permission to bury him. This being contemptuously granted, the body was fastened to a cart and transported across the water to her house in the New Town of Ayr. With warm water she washed away the filth and finding still a flickering of the heart spooned into him warm milk, and at last he opened his eyes. On a raised couch, draped about with tapestry to shield him from view, with great care and vigilance the nurse and her daughter secretly nursed him back to health.

Thomas Rimour,[12] spending some time with the minister of nearby Faile Monastery and hearing from him all that had happened, was deeply concerned that this young man of good blood should have been starved to death in prison, for William's stand against the English had already won him a reputation. A servant present in the market when the body was cast over the wall was sent for and asked to repeat what he had seen. Thomas hurried to the nurse's house for confirmation of the story and, bursting in, saw the man upon the couch. Believing the English had discovered the secret, the woman pleaded with the stranger to forget, but Thomas must see with his own eyes, alive, 'him that all has wrought'. With glad greetings the two men conversed. Thomas, already famous for his prophecies, made another that was to catch the imagination of Scots and English alike, uplifting the former and weighing heavily on the minds of the latter:

'"For sooth, ere he decease
Shall many thousands in the field make end.
From Scotland he shall forth the Southron send;
And Scotland thrice he shall bring to the peace.
So good of hand again shall ne'er be kenned."'
*[Book I, lines 346–350]*

Into his mother's care at Ellerslie William sent his good nurse, her daughter and child, and a servant, setting off himself for Riccarton with an old rusty sword found in the house. On the way he encountered one Squire Longcastle with two attendants, and drew aside to let them pass. The Englishman ordered him to bide, accusing him as a thief or spy. Pleading sickness, William prayed to be left alone, but Longcastle drew a sword, pronouncing him a sturdy knave who should accompany him back to Ayr. With his rusty blade the

Scot slew all three, and taking horses, weapons and 'all they had' rode in haste to Riccarton. There he was warmly received by Sir Richard and his sons. There too came his mother, 'gud Robert Boyd' and other friends, all overjoyed at his escape and recovery. The nurse, passing Corsbie, imparted the good news to Sir Reginald and his three sons, and the sheriff hurried to Riccarton. Harry finely depicts the emotional meeting.

But for the presence of 'Lord Percy', stated so positively by the Minstrel, these earlier adventures could be spread over the period 1292–1296 without seeming 'fabulous'. Curiously, Percy is designated, even today, the 'nephew' of John de Warenne, Earl of Surrey. But the Sir Henry de Percy[13] who crossed into Scotland with King Edward in March 1296 was in fact the Earl's grandson. His father, also Sir Henry, who died in 1272, in 1268 married Alienora (Eleanor), Warenne's second daughter. Henry was their third and only surviving son. The powerful Lord of Northumberland, he may have supported Edward at Norham and Upsettlington in 1291, but it is unlikely that he held any authority in Scotland at that time, when he would be but eighteen or nineteen years of age. He almost certainly accompanied the King on his progress through Scotland in 1296 and, as we have seen, was appointed Warden of Galloway and Ayr on 8 September, arriving in the district in October.[14] Was he preceded in the post by another relative, or is this one of Harry's 'serious errors', assuming the earlier presence of Percy on the certainty of the later appointment? Without dates, any chronological order of events is impossible. It is only when Wallace's early exploits, his imprisonment, illness and recovery are assigned to the period autumn 1296 to spring 1297 that they become 'incredible'.

Let us see how the Minstrel introduces his hero. He opens the first of his twelve 'Buiks' with a remonstrance, that 'we let o'er slide the noble worthy deeds of our ancestors', honouring instead 'our enemies that come of Saxon blood'.

> 'We read of one right famous of renowne
> Of worthy blood that reigns in this region:
> And henceforth I will my process hold
> Of Willyam Wallas you have heard been told.
> His forebears that likes to understand
> Of whole linage, and true line of Scotland.'
>
> *[Book I, lines 17–22]*

Dealing with Wallace's parentage he then goes on –

'But Malcolm got upon this lade bright
Schir Malcolm Wallas, a full gentle knight;
And William also, as chronicles bear on hand,
Which after was the rescue of Scotland.'
*[Book I, lines 35–38]*

Then follows a revue of events from the death of Alexander III, the sack of Berwick, and the dethroning of King John in July 1296.

'I may not now put all their deeds in thyme.
Of chronicle why should I tarry lang?
To Wallace agayne now briefly I will gang.
Scotland was lost when he was but a child,
And o'er set through with our enemies wild.
His father Malcolm to the Lennox fled;
His eldest son thither with him he led.'
*[Book I, lines 142–148]*

Now, is Harry saying that the flight and subsequent happenings took place after Baliol, or is he reverting back to the first surrender in 1291, when Wallace was 'but a child' of seventeen or so? Is it really conceivable – if indeed he was outlawed in 1292 – that he would have remained at peace and retirement under the tyranny King John's reign did little to relieve? The break-up of his home, the death of his father, and the persecution and exile of his mother, filled his heart with bitter hatred, and set his mind to reprisal and revenge. We learn of his distress and uneasiness at the plight of his country; how no Englishman ever crossed his path alone and lived to tell the tale; how some disappeared 'but none wist by what way' and for their own protection went about in groups, probably of five, since this number is one frequently encountered in Harry's narrative.

'In those hard days' says Murison, 'the removal of an enemy did not touch the conscience as it does in modern civilised society . . . and the justification derived from intolerable oppression is, at any rate, a vastly more efficient salve in the actual case than it is in mere historical contemplation. While we may deplore, we need not be so childishly unhistorical as to effect not to understand.'[15]

The claim that there was no reason for Sir Malcolm or his son –

or any other – to come up against the English, 'that no blow was struck before 1296',[16] is not consistent with fact. By the middle of 1295 the country was in ferment. The Council of Twelve had taken over government and the Franco-Scottish Alliance, signed by King Philip in October, was ratified by King John at Dunfermline on 23 February 1296, 'with the assent, not only of his prelates and nobles, but also of the chief burgh corporations and other public bodies of the kingdom'.[17] If Wallace cannot be connected with affairs at Berwick in March, and Dunbar in April, his renewed activity was surely their outcome, the removal of King John three months later the final spur to his resolution.

In the Laglane Woods he was sustained by relatives. From his life as an outlaw 'his body was hardened against all changes of fortune, his mind strengthened to deeds of greater daring'.[18] Whether or not he devised a plan of action against his enemies, he must at some time have gathered together his growing band of supporters and begun to shape them into a disciplined force, when he 'buckled on his armour' and the youth became the man.

# Chapter IV

'Joyous July' had passed when Wallace left Riccarton, accompanied by Sir Richard's eldest son Adam, 'large of person and eighteen years of age'. There was Edward Little, 'his sister's son'; Robert Boyd; and Kneland, a 'near cousin', all wearing light armour. Ever since his imprisonment at Ayr, so Harry tells us, Wallace wore 'good sure weid'. A 'habergoine' was worn under his gown, made of chain mail to protect the breast and neck, with a collar of steel in his doublet; there was a 'capleyne' or steel lining in his cap or bonnet, and his face was bare. Gloves of plaited cloth covered the wrists, the arms and legs encased in boiled leather, with knee-plates of iron and guards for the shins. He would carry a shield, decorated perhaps with his personal device, the red lion; a dagger for close-quarter fighting; and the two-handed sword.[1]

Friends and retainers armed with spears and pikes increased the number to fifty, and brought to Wallace news that greatly pleased him. A convoy was passing from Carlisle to Ayr led by Fenwick, the officer who commanded the English when Sir Malcolm was slain. Resolved to avenge the death of his father, Wallace rode to Loudoun Hill and camped overnight in a wood. A hosteller supplied the company with meat and drink, and information as to the position of the convoy. 'In the gray dawning' the Scots built a dyke of stones to narrow the approach of the English horsemen. The sun was breaking through when they came in sight, Fenwick in flittering gear on a great horse. He saw the Scots, and, concluding that their leader was the outlaw 'that escaped our prison', advanced with 180 men, never for a moment doubting their superiority over a handful of foot-troops. Standing shoulder to shoulder and keeping close order, the Scots spearmen defied all attempts to break their ranks, and a hundred English were killed, Wallace himself striking at Fenwick, who fell on the far side of his horse, to be finished off by Boyd. Eighty English escaped and fled to Ayr to report to (Sir Henry) Percy, and the entire convoy of provisions fell to the Scots. For the first time, pikemen on foot discovered that armed mounted troops were not invincible. This skilful and daring exploit gave weight to the prophecy of Thomas, fame to the name of Wallace, and hope to the downtrodden people.

Percy's council recommended that Wallace be restrained through the medium of his uncle, Sir Reginald, who should be held responsible for his good behaviour. A bond was drawn up, and the sheriff sought out his nephew in Clydesdale Forest, where the spoils of the convoy were being distributed. On the advice of those closest to him, and to safeguard his uncle, Wallace agreed to ten months' peace, beginning in August. Each man then returned to his own home, William going with Sir Reginald to Corsbie.

A party of fifteen took themselves one day to Ayr, Wallace with his face covered to avoid recognition. An Englishman at play with sword and buckler jeeringly invited him to try the sword. "Smyte on," he said, "I defy thine action." Wallace accepted the challenge and smote him through to the shoulders. As Harry puts it, "What need for wordis more!" A fight ensued with many casualties, but Percy, realising that his own men were in part to blame, merely bound the sheriff to keep his nephew away from market towns and fairs – a surprisingly lenient attitude if indeed three of Percy's 'near kin' were among those slain. The Minstrel represents Sir Henry as the most reasonable and courteous of the English governors, one who at least acknowledged Wallace's skill, strength, and prowess. Had he been King Edward's man, mused Percy, Scotland could be broken, and 'the whole empyr he mycht have conquest then'.

As to why such a troublesome youngster was allowed to remain at large, Dr Rogers offers a theory: the Priest of Dunipace would have his home at Torwood Castle, seat of the wealthy Umfravilles, a family of considerable influence in both countries. Edward's cautious conciliation towards such families would provide protection automatically for the priest's pupil.[2] Be that as it may, on returning to Corsbie and being shown the latest communication concerning him, Wallace promised he would do nothing further to endanger his uncle while residing under his roof.

In September, a great council was summoned at Glasgow under Bishop Bek; and Sheriff Craufurd of Ayr duly set out, taking his nephew with him. With the sumpter-horse in the lead, Wallace and two companions rode ahead, soon overtaking Percy's baggage-train. One of its horses, loaded with riches and provisions, was exhausted and could go no further, five armed men being left in charge. Their conductor immediately appropriated the Scot's supply horse, insolently cutting the traces when they ascertained to whom it belonged. Remembering the bond and his promise, Wallace, while expressing his indignation at the robbery in time of truce, stayed his hand, and rode back to inform the sheriff. Sir Reginald had submitted to King Edward, probably in 1291, and had been confirmed in his hereditary office by the King on 14 May 1296; the embarrassment of his position will be readily appreciated. Fearing the consequences of retaliation, to himself and his family, and having anyway lost his horse and supplies, the sheriff deemed it prudent to remain where he was, at the travellers' hostelry at the Mearns. Peace or no peace, Wallace determined on revenge, and, renouncing his obligation to his uncle, rode off again with Gray and Kerlie. They caught up with Percy's train, engaged and killed the five attendants, and taking spoil, horses and harness, passed into the Lennox.

When this news reached the council, a now enraged Percy ordered the sheriff before an assize, but being at the Mearns he could not be implicated in any way, as he was in ignorance of the movements of his relative. He was made to swear to have no further friendly communication with him; and, for his actions against the English, William Wallace was again outlawed.

In the Lennox, held by Earl Malcolm, were many men still in defiance of the King of England. The Earl had twice sworn fealty 'but had not then made band'. He made Wallace welcome, and would have had him master of his house and estate if he would stay in the district. Wallace expressed his gratitude but declined the offer, it being inconsistent with his plans to drive the English from the whole of Scotland. All who joined him of their own free will he accepted, and sixty men

'Before the Earl, all with a good accord,
And him received as captain and their lord.'
*[Book IV, lines 191–192]*

One of the favourite accusations hurled against Wallace is of the 'rabble' he gathered about him, and undoubtedly some were rough characters. Desperate fugitives attached themselves to him, and men like Kerlie, whose circumstances were similar to his own. Some were Irish exiles; one valuable recruit, Steven of Ireland – though Harry says 'he born war of Argyll' – struck up a firm friendship with Kerlie, Wallace's most trusted adherent. Another was 'a big dour fellow . . . with a sad and sorrowful countenance' named Fawdoun. Of his old party, Wallace had now only the parson Gray, and Kerlie. These stalwarts he instructed to remain close to his person, and with this small army, late in 1296, he rode out through the Lennox to the north, to wage war against the English.

They had for a start the spoil of Percy's train with which to launch a campaign. The peel at Gargunnock, near Stirling, was observed to be lightly guarded, with the drawbridge left down and the sentinel asleep. They crossed unhindered, but found the peel door secured by a strong bar which resisted all attempts to remove it. Considerably annoyed at the delay, Wallace set about it himself and, to the marvel of his men, by sheer strength of arm wrenched the bar free, bringing down with it three yards of masonry. The noise aroused the sentinel, and the captain, Thirlwall, with his garrison of twenty-two, was soon up in arms. All were slain, their women and children spared. First destroying the building, the raiders took the supplies and anything of value to a nearby wood. Moss made the going too treacherous for horses, but move on they must, and with Steven acting as guide proceeded on foot, crossing the Forth and making for Methven Wood. The forest was abundantly stocked with deer, and the party made an excellent meal. Here they could remain while Wallace, with seven men, next day made a reconnaissance of St Johnston. The provost asked his name; "Will Malcolmson," (son of Malcolm) Wallace replied, and his business, he said, was to seek for himself a better dwelling. The provost explained that he must question strangers, not from any discourtesy, but because of rumours that were rife about the outlaw, Wallace. The visitor had heard tell of that man, but could give no tidings. He was allowed to pass into the town, where he planned to stay a few days.

He soon discovered the English dispositions, regretful that his own small force could not take the town. Having learnt, however, that soldiers from St Johnston were being sent under Sir James Butler to fortify Kinclaven Castle, he hastened to Methven Wood. A blast on his horn quickly assembled his men, and all was made ready for the march to Kinclaven. Positioning his troops in a wooded hollow, Wallace bided his time until sure of the English train, which proved to be of ninety men, mounted and heavily armed. Believing, as did the horsemen at Loudoun Hill, that the Scots could be quickly mowed down, these were taught the same lesson, and sixty were killed. The English fought gallantly until outnumbered, and with their commander dead they fled to the castle. With his customary speed, Wallace reached the gate at the same time, and friend and foe went through together. Every fighting man was killed, the castle plundered and set on fire. Lady Butler, her children, the women and priests, spared and set free, hurried to Sir Gerard Heron, Captain of St Johnston.

Six companies, 1,000 men in all, were ordered to pursue Wallace. Sir John Butler, son of Sir James whom he 'clove to the teeth' in the fight, was to lead the attack. The Scots took up a strong position which their leader determined must be held if they were to contain Butler's 150 archers against his twenty. Five constructions, made from the branches of trees, he erected as baffles against enemy horses and archers; a sixth they could retire behind if the need arose. An English archer, observing where he came into the open to draw his bow, shot an arrow that caught him in the neck, under the left side of the chin, through the collar of steel. Wallace killed him instantly. In the desperate battle that raged, he 'cast all ways to save his men from the death'. When his own supply of arrows was shot he fought with his hands to protect his men, for 'no man was there that Wallace's bow might draw'.

In the afternoon the English were reinforced by a further 300 under Sir William Loraine, nephew of Sir James Butler. Assailed on three sides, Wallace was forced to retire further into the dense but narrow wood. He got close enough to make a strike at Sir John Butler, who, although brought to the ground, was saved by the bough of a tree, and was carried off by his men. Loraine then closed in. All his fine armour was no protection against the deft hand of Wallace, springing out from the trees to cut him down. The Scots rallied round their leader and won through to a new 'strength'. While Heron moved all his troops to one position, Wallace retreated to Cargill Wood, 'thanking great God'. He had lost but seven men, the English 120. Two nights later the Scots returned to collect the buried spoils of Kinclaven, which Heron's men had sought in vain.

It was during his first sojourn at St Johnston that Wallace took as his mistress a young woman 'of great beauty', and in disguise now returned to visit her. In spite of his caution he was recognised and his movements reported to Sir Gerard Heron, before whom the woman was brought. She at first denied all knowledge of Wallace, but offered the alternatives of death by burning, or riches and marriage to a knight of her own choosing, she disclosed the time of her lover's next appointment. Armed men were set to watch, and Wallace came, but, uneasy about his men, could not be persuaded to stay the night. Fearing her fate at the hands of the English if the plan should go wrong, the woman broke down and confessed what she had done. Wallace forgave her and sent her away; and, arraying himself in her garments, passed safely through the south gate of the town. He came up against some soldiers and in an assumed voice directed them to the house where, he said, Wallace's 'leman' had him locked in. But two of the guards followed him, suspicious of the increased pace of this 'stalwart quean'. At the South Inch he turned to slay them both, and made haste to Elcho Park where his men were camped.

The two bodies marked the passage of his flight, and Heron next surrounded the wood with 300 men, again sending Butler to make the attack. In the first onslaught, Wallace lost fifteen of his forty. Cutting through the enemy to the banks of the Tay, they found the water too deep to cross. As only a few could swim there was no choice but to turn and face Butler, to 'do or die', and Wallace lost another nine. While the English were re-forming, the Scots made a lightning dash between their camps, making for Gask Wood, an uphill journey of two miles. They had gone but a short distance when the surly Fawdoun 'broke down' and neither persuasion nor argument could move him on. He was suspected of treachery, and rather than allow him to endanger the lives of the rest, Wallace angrily struck off his head. Heron had with him a trained sleuth-hound. It stopped on scenting the dead man and as the English gathered round, Steven and Kerlie mingled among them, the latter striking Heron dead, and the two escaped to the wood.

Wallace's party, now reduced to fourteen, occupied Gask Hall. Harry tells of his fatigue and mental excitement, his anxiety for his two good men, his troubled conscience over Fawdoun; how he hears bugle calls and sends men out in relays to investigate; how, when he was alone, the apparition of Fawdoun appeared, head in hand, and caused him 'greatly aghast' to leap fifteen feet over a closed stairway to escape from the Hall, set on fire he believed by the vengeful ghost. Making his way alone along the banks of the Earn, in the gloom and mist he encountered another party under Sir John Butler, returning from a watch on the fords. The wanderer's explanation of his business Butler suspected, and he drew his sword. The Scot cut him down and seizing his horse rode furiously away, hotly pursued by Butler's men. As the leaders caught up he struck them down also, leaving twenty dead in his wake. At Blackford the horse collapsed and Wallace proceeded on foot 'through the long heather'. Reaching the Forth before dawn he swam the cold river and made for Torwood, where he found shelter with a widow and her three sons. Two tended and guarded him while he slept, concealed in a thicket, while the third went for the Priest of Dunipace. He came, and, beckoned into the hiding where Wallace lay, observed how easily a vexed wife could destroy him!

A woman sent to Gask Hall for tidings of his men – lured into a trap, he feared, by the bugle calls – returned that night and told of the trail of dead men, but of his own supporters there was no sign, and at the Hall not a stone misplaced – circumstances that impressed further on the mind of Wallace some supernatural influence. Modern logic will recognise delirium in his fevered imagination, aggravated most likely by the arrow wound in his neck, by days of strenuous fighting, and nights on the move without food or rest.

'"What I have had in war before this day –
Prison and pain – to this night was but play . . .
*[Book V, lines 381–382]*

'"I moan far more the losing of my men
Than for myself, had I ten times such pain."'
*[Book V, lines 387–388]*

Percy's men meanwhile, believing the outlaw to have drowned in the Forth, reported to their lord that they had waited, expectant but in vain, for the body to pass under Stirling Bridge. Recounting the great strength of Wallace and his knowledge of the river, Percy refused to believe him dead:

'"He is on life, that shall our nation feel."'
*[Book V, line 514]*

The Priest tried to persuade his nephew to seek King Edward's peace, to accept a lordship and lands, not to risk his life in an apparently hopeless struggle, since he had now lost all his men. Reminding the Priest that it was he who had instilled in him a passion for freedom and liberty:

'"Uncle" said Wallace, "of such words no more.
This is but eking of my trouble sore.
Better I like to see the Southron de
Than land or gold that they can give to me.
Believe right well, from war I will not cease
Till time that I bring Scotland to the peace,
Or die therefor: that plainly understand."'
*[Book V, lines 395–401]*

News of their leader's whereabouts reached Steven and Kerlie, who joined him, and the three friends 'wept for perfect joy' at finding each other alive. Refreshed and rested, Wallace prepared to move off. The Priest, seeing his determination, provided horses and gear, the widow some silver and two of her sons.

Arriving at Dundaff in Stirlingshire, the five were made extremely welcome by the lord, Sir John the Graham. A younger Sir John was present and eager to join the little band of patriots but Wallace would not take him then. Now, the old knight could not have been John's father; *he* was Sir David Graham and died about 1270 leaving three sons. The eldest, Sir Patrick, died valiantly at the Battle of Dunbar, where the youngest, Sir David, was taken prisoner. Anyhow, as the Minstrel tells it, 'before the old knight, on a broad shield' the second son, Sir John, and Wallace each swore an oath to be true to the other, the latter promising to send for John when the time was right. At least two and possibly several years older than Wallace, he was to become his great friend and illustrious 'rycht hand'.

Over the Christmas of this year 1296, Wallace stayed at Gilbank, an estate of the Stewards held by Auchinlek, a youth of nineteen married to a Craufurd lady.[3] Kerlie carried messages to Sir Reginald at Corsbie, Adam Wallace at Riccarton, to Robert Boyd and John Blair. Family and friends visited Wallace, all contributing cash and kind to the cause.

An Englishman, Sir William de Heselrigg, was Sheriff of Lanark when, according to Harry, Wallace met Marion Braidfute, only surviving child of Sir Hugh Braidfute of Lamington. Her parents dead, her brother recently slain by Heselrigg, she now had the heritage, and had been selected by that sheriff as a suitable wife for his son.

'Amiable and benign she was, and wise:
Courteous and sweet, fulfilled of gentrice.
Her tongue well ruled, her face right fresh and fair;
Withall she was a maid of virtue rare.
Humbly her led, and purchased a good name;
And kept herself with every wight from blame.
True rightwise folk a great favour her lent;
Upon a day as to the kirk she went.'
*[Book V, lines 597–604]*

It was in the church that Wallace first saw her, his admiration soon deepening into love. Resolved as he was to fight for his country's freedom, and being outlawed by her enemies, he hesitated to pursue the course of love and marriage. Marion, who was eighteen, returned his affection, and she needed protection from the offensive attentions of the Heselriggs, 'but leman [mistress] she would be to no man born'. At secret meetings they declared their love and made some sort of bond. If the kingdom were free, William would gladly marry, but at this time must give his all to the task he had undertaken, and he took his leave.

For a while he stayed away from the town, that war might prove the stronger claim. He had sampled 'the foolishness of love' with the false leman in St Johnston and his behaviour there had brought confusion to his men. Yet 'the lusty payne of luff' persisted, causing him to argue the case with his friend. Kerlie, knowing his torment, counselled marriage. The Minstrel is at his poetic best in these passages, handling the affair with touching delicacy. It was one April 'when woodis have won their worthy weid of greyne' that Wallace returned to Lanark and his love. Legend has it that they were married at St Kentigern's, and had a house near the Castlegate. Harry, whose authority we may recall is Wallace's clerical companion John Blair, affirms:

'Beginning band, with witnesses beside,
Mine auctor says she was his rightwise wife.

Now live in peace, now leave in good accord!
Now live in bliss, now leave in whole pleasance!
For she by choice has both her love and lord.'
*[Book VI, lines 47–51]*

How long this state of bliss continued Harry declares himself unable to say, but a daughter was born to them. This would place the marriage probably earlier, but no later than the summer of 1296. Their daughter is said to have married a squire named Shaw, 'and right good men came of this lady young'. An edition of Harry's poem printed in 1594 inserts lines not found in the original manuscript, alleging a second marriage, to Sir William Baillie of Hoprig, their heirs succeeding to the lands of Lamington.

Dr. Rogers, however, will have none of it. He states, rather forcibly, 'the entire narrative is baseless; the Patriot died unmarried, nor does he seem to have had any illegitimate offspring.'[4] Paterson notes that 'Hugh Braidfoot of Lamington in the shire of Lanark, died about 1295'[5] but he fails to give his authority; and Murison states that 'Sir William Baillie,[6] second of Hoprig, as son-in-law of Sir William Seton, obtained a charter of 'Lambiston' barony in 1368.[7]

None of this seems conclusive proof against the marriage. It would be comforting to know that William did wed his Marion, that there was some sweetness in their troubled life, but the matter rests entirely on the statement of the Minstrel, and presumably his 'auctor' John Blair.

No 'Braidfute' appears in documents or records of the time. Tradition accepts what history may not, and events will show, in relation to the ultimate fate of Sir William de Heselrigg, that these Braidfutes present an extenuating factor, and it would be surprising indeed if, after the death of Wallace, any record of their existence escaped Edward's meticulous scrutiny. On the subject of Scottish records and muniments, Dr. Lingard notes: 'It is indeed true that no records of an earlier date than the reign of Robert I exist in Scotland; but neither do they exist in England. The probability is that they perished in 1661, when, by command of Charles II, the records brought from Scotland under the Commonwealth were sent back by sea, and eighty-five hogsheads of papers were lost in a ship that foundered.'[8]

# Chapter V

After the Christmas of 1296 Wallace and his party rode into Annandale, to be joined there by his nephews, Tom Halliday and Edward Little. With these two and Kerlie, he ventured into Lochmaben, a town he had long wished to see.[1] Harry describes vividly the chain of events: first ordering dinner at a hostelry, they left their horses and went to hear Mass. The Warden of the eastern districts was Sir Robert de Clifford. His son arrived at the hostel with four companions, and demanded of the 'gyd wyff' whose were the horses outside. Knowing his disposition she replied cautiously that they belonged to some gentlemen who had ridden in from the west. Clifford and his men spitefully cut off the tails of the four horses, leaving them to bleed. When the Scots returned and discovered the cruel and wanton act, Wallace mounted and rode swiftly after the Englishmen. Although greatly enraged, in jocular vein he called out his thanks for services rendered 'without command of me':

> '"Reward agayne, me think, I should pay thee;
> Since I of late now come out of the west
> In this country, a barber of the best:
> To cut and shave, and that a wonder gud,
> Now though shall feel how I use to let blud."'
> *[Book V, lines 756–760]*

And so saying he 'ended young Clifford's career' and one other, while his men dealt with the rest. Without waiting to dine they paid the landlady for her trouble and departed, to rejoin the remainder of their party in the Knock Wood. It was small, offering little protection, and the mutilated horses were failing through loss of blood. The Scots dismounted and led their steeds to higher ground. An English force of seven score, sent out to cut them down, could be seen a mile away, bright armour shining. Their fresh horses soon gained on the Scots and two of Wallace's men were severely wounded by the oncoming bowmen. Angrily he turned and, fighting desperately, killed fifteen of those foremost, the rest falling back to the main body. Tom Halliday sighted a further 200 English in ambush and advised his uncle to withdraw. This he did, pursued by the enemy under the esteemed warrior Sir Hugh de Moreland. Waiting under a huge oak, Wallace cut through the steel-clad knight with one stroke of his two-handed sword, and mounting Moreland's 'noble courser' in place of his own injured one, charged into the fray. The battle continued with such fury that the English were compelled to retire, with the loss of twenty men. Sir John de Graystock, recently arrived from England, took command, jeering at the troops for fleeing in the face of so small a band. With 300 men he rode after the Scots, ignoring advice from some who knew better than to do so. Wallace, unwilling to expose his few to battle on the plain, coolly led them on, taking turns with Halliday to guard the rear.

Sir John Graham with thirty followers was riding near Queensferry, hoping for tidings of Wallace. He met up with a 'near' relative of Lady Wallace, Kirkpatrick of Torthorwold, who with his supporters had been six months in Eskdale Wood holding out against King Edward. Joining forces the two parties gladly reinforced their countrymen in a fresh charge, causing much slaughter in the enemy lines, Wallace on foot with his two-handed sword 'making gret rowme about hym'. A hundred of the English held together but Graystock fled. Finding Graham mounted and cutting down at random any of the enemy he encountered, Wallace sharply ordered him to pursue the flying chieftain, it being his policy always to strike at the leader. At the Knock Head Graham overtook and killed Graystock.[2] The rout was complete. After the battle, when the Scots leaders came together, Wallace apologised to Sir John for the brusqueness of the order, given in the heat of fighting, and received an equally generous response.

The Scots next took possession of Lochmaben Castle, seat of the Bruce. English forces that had been engaged at the Knock Head, seeking shelter in the castle and unaware that it had fallen, were slain as they entered. Crawford Castle followed, after another bloody skirmish. All fighting men were killed, the women and children spared, 'according to Wallace's invariable rule'.[3] Speed and surprise were the elements he favoured, his knowledge of the terrain ensuring always a safe retreat. These methods notched up for the patriots a series of victories, establishing them – in the eyes of the common people at least – as the foremost defenders of their freedom.

In May of this year 1297, Wallace with nine men proceeded to Lanark, to join his wife at their house at the Castlegate. There too came Sir John Graham with fifteen followers. As Marion had refused the sheriff's son in favour of Wallace, a conflict was inevitable. Heselrigg arranged for him to be insulted by an English soldier, 'the starkest man he knew'. Returning from Mass, decked out in fashionable green garb, the Scots strolled along, engaging in friendly argument with one another. The soldier greeted them in mock salute: "Since ye ar Scottis . . .". In the ribald exchange Wallace gave as good as he got. Derisory remarks about his 'goodly greyne', even a gesture towards his sword he endured with unusual patience. Not wanting a disturbance he tried to get away, but Heselrigg and Sir Robert Thorn, the Captain of Lanark, were immediately on hand with 200 armed men.

The conflict was 'rycht awful, hard and strong'. Taken at such disadvantage the Scots were forced to seek shelter, Wallace and Graham holding back the enemy till their men were safe. 'The woman' says Harry, seeing their peril, lifted the gate to allow them through her premises, engaging the pursuers in argument till they got away to the safety of Cartland Crags.

For this the brave girl paid with her life, being inhumanely slaughtered by the enraged soldiers.

'When Southrons saw that escaped was Wallace
Again they turned, the woman tuk on case,
Put her to ded, I can noght tell you how!
Of such matter I may not tarry now.'
*[Book VI, lines 191–194]*

News of his wife's death was brought to Wallace by her servant; his grief, and that of his close friends, Graham among them, was 'extreme'. Young Auchinlek hearing the news, with ten men went at once to his kinsman's side in Cartland Woods. Seeing their distress, Wallace pulled himself together:

' "We can noght now choose her life again. . . .
*[Book VI, line 210]*

"Sir John" he said, "let all this mourning be.
And for her sake there shall ten thousand de.
Where men may weep their courage is the less."'
*[Book VI, lines 221–223]*

That such an incident as Harry describes did take place is borne out by Andrew of Wyntoun. He refers to Wallace's 'leman', 'a plesand fayre woman'; and he says that the sheriff came to Lanark after the disturbance and had her put to death.

'The king of Inglandis lutenand
Come to Lanark; and there he
Gert this woman taken be
And gert her soon be put to dede
That Wallace saw in that stead
In hiding where he stood near by;
Therefor in heart he was heavy.'[4]

At night some thirty Scots entered the town of Lanark by different gates, so as not to arouse suspicion, Wallace hiding in a loft, says Wyntoun, and waiting till after midnight to approach the sheriff's house. He kicked down the door, calling, "Here am I, Will the Waleys."[5] Heselrigg rushed to the stair, spear in hand, but he was no match for the mood of Wallace, who got him by the throat, stabbed him and hurled him down the high stair. Auchinlek fell over the body and to make sure he was dead stabbed him twice more. Young Heselrigg, coming to the aid of his father, was similarly dispatched. Graham meanwhile had gone to the house of Sir Robert Thorn, which he fired, killing all the inhabitants. The townspeople, brought out on the streets by the din and burning, rallied to the assistance of Wallace, eagerly grasping the opportunity to rid themselves of Edward's tyrannical minions. All were driven out or destroyed, ending English domination in the area.

Harry appears to have borrowed Wyntoun's precise words for the first part of this episode. Did he then turn back to his 'auctor' Blair for a more detailed account, or is he taking a minstrel's licence with the facts? In either case the woman is there. While it is still fashionable to discredit the Minstrel, to 'write out' of his script anything that cannot be otherwise substantiated, Wyntoun's version of the incident – written at most two generations away from it –

cannot be so lightly cast aside. His *Orygynale Cronykil of Scotland* is, however, part of a World History and as such is less concerned with particulars than Blair's and Harry's; in any case, the two versions are not totally irreconcilable. Allowing for some romantic embellishment, Wallace's reaction to the deed is at least suggestive that 'the woman' was dear to him, rather than someone casual who gave help and shelter. She must have had a name, she would have lived in a house, and under the circumstances recorded would have become a legendary if not an historic figure before Blind Harry's time. The point of argument for or against Wallace's 'wife' is obvious enough.

Burton, at least, finds the first part of the story – that of the murder of a wife – 'not on the whole improbable'. The second part he shows to be confirmed sixty years later. A Northumbrian knight, Sir Thomas de Gray, imprisoned by the Scots in Edinburgh Castle and writing a world history,[6] 'fortunately gave disproportionate prominence to events . . . in which he or his father participated'.[7] In May 1297 the senior knight was at Lanark during the uprising. He was seriously wounded, and left on the street for dead. A fortunate chance saved him from death through exposure – he lay between two burning buildings until found by a comrade, Sir William de Lundy, who attended his recovery.

Until these events at Lanark, Harry's is the only testimony to the early career of Wallace, and there can be few who would accept it unreservedly. Yet in some instances Harry's versions are given credence over the chronicles of the monks – themselves not averse, as Burton remarks, 'to do services by forgery and falsification'.[8] In the preparation of this book, not one has been found that did not refer to or quote at length from the traditional chronicle of the despised Minstrel. Even the sceptical Lord Hailes may have been glad to retract some of his 'absolute rejections' had he lived a century later.

Likewise, the early struggles of Bruce – his exile, hardships and privations on the way to the throne – derive mostly from the poem *The Bruce* by John Barbour, Archdeacon of Aberdeen, which was more readily acceptable than Harry's because it was composed within living memory of King Robert and its author was a learned man.

But in May 1297 Wallace enters recorded history, and the placing in wrong sequence by some writers of the sack of Berwick in

March 1296, and Lanark, as if the former was Edward's just reprisal for the latter, is inexcusable carelessness. This last event is known to history as the Lanark Rising or the Rise of Wallace, when William, his family avenged, first drew his sword in the name of his lawful if unworthy king. Wyntoun records:

'And this Willame thai made thare
Oure same cheftane and leddare.
For he durst well tak on hand
Wyth that he fayre wes, and plesand.
Manlyk, stowte, and liberale,
And wys in all gud governale.
To sla he sparyd nought Inglismen
Til Scottis he dyd gret profyt then.'

A leader had arisen, 'a man of compassion and love towards his countrymen'[9] who asked nothing of them that he had not or would not himself endure, and who developed a strength of character without parallel in his time. In this man, and in him alone in those dark days, could the Scottish people place their trust, their hope, and, in their unquenchable desire to remain a free nation, their destiny. He did not fail them. With nothing but his sword, his indomitable courage, and his steadfast belief in the rightness of his cause, William Wallace 'lifted up his head'.[10]

# Chapter VI

'At the same time there was in Scotland a certain young man (juvenis) William le Walays by name, an archer, who sought his food with bow and quiver, born and brought up in the very dregs of society, even among outlaws. He having, as is the way of mighty men, proved his boldness in many places . . .'

This is how Wallace first appears in one ancient English manuscript.

In another:[1] 'there was a certain public robber, William Waleys by name, who had been outlawed. Finding himself a vagabond, he gathered together . . .'[2]

Scots writers, of course, see him very differently. Some idea of his impact may be gathered – again from Wyntoun:

'Twelve hundred ninety year and seven
Frae Christ was born, the King of heaven
William Wallace in Clydisdale
That saw his kyn supressed hail.

It is not at all difficult to understand how, in the superstitious climate of the day, he should come to be looked upon as some heaven-sent deliverer, or that he should believe himself to be one. That very fatefulness of which Lord Rosebery speaks, recognisable in its day, and building onto an already established reputation of courage and resolve, brought the 'wholly supressed' people flocking to his standard. Soon Wallace found himself at the head of 3,000 horsemen and a vast concourse on foot.

One most welcome recruit was a man 'of gret statur and sum part gray'. Born at Riccarton and much travelled in England and France as a pursuivant in the service of King Edward, he had, so

Harry says, always refused to bear arms. He was probably one of the force sent to England by Alexander III to assist his father-in-law in his quarrel with the barons. Gilbert de Grimmesby carried the sacred banner of St John of Beverley for Edward, a service for which the King on 13 October 1296 directed Earl Warenne, the Governor of Scotland, to find him a living worth 20 marks a year.[3] His wide knowledge and military experience he now offered to Wallace, whom he found in Kyle. The English called him 'but Grymmesbe'. Wallace's men:

> 'Thai turnyt hys name, frae tyme that thai hym knew
> And callit hym Jop; off ingen he was trew.
> In all hys tyme gud service in hym found,
> Gave hym to ber the armes of Scotland.'
> *[Book VI, lines 315–318]*

He may have carried the colour for Wallace in those early days after Lanark, but the service was soon to be provided by Alexander Scrymgeour, the royal standard-bearer, according to Buchanan an office long established.[4] The two are sometimes taken to be one and the same.

The greatest support was to come from the lairds and small farmers, and the peasants who worked the productive lands of the south, their livelihood and very means of existence trampled underfoot or confiscated to feed the English army and its horses. The nobles, to whom the people would naturally turn, were too taken up with their own interests, fighting one another, swearing or retracting allegiance to Edward as and when expedient – Robert Bruce, the young Earl of Carrick, being a notable example. Born in 1274 he was the grandson of the 5th Lord of Annandale, the Competitor for the throne in 1291. His mother, Marjorie, the Celtic Countess of Carrick in her own right, bestowed that Earldom on her husband, Robert Bruce, 6th Lord of Annandale. At Baliol's accession the title and estate of Carrick were assigned to young Robert, making him one of the most influential lords in the land. Edward is said to have promised the throne to the Competitor if he would assist in removing Baliol; the old Bruce died in 1295. After the Battle of Dunbar in 1296, his son, reminding Edward of his promise, received the reply in French: "Have we nothing else to do than to conquer kingdoms for you?"[5] The King's rejection of their claim the House of Bruce bitterly resented, and with the removal of King John considered themselves the rightful heirs. The 6th Lord retired to England, leaving the defence of their Scottish heritage to his five lively sons. He died in 1304.

The most powerful family in Scotland were the Comyns. In the declining years of Alexander II and the minority of Alexander III, they all but ruled the kingdom. In an effort to reduce their power their enemies sought advice from the King of England and Henry, out of affection for his son-in-law, travelled north to the Border. The 'judicious alterations and useful statutes' there enacted were disregarded by the Comyns; they kidnapped the boy king and continued with their own policies. Their 'reign' came to an end when Walter, the head of the family, died from poison believed to have been administered by his English wife. When Alexander III came of age, the family made humble submission and received his pardon. Alternate generations were known as the Black and the Red. Sir John Comyn, Lord of Badenoch, the Black Comyn who withdrew his claim to the throne in 1291, was married to Baliol's sister. It was their son, Sir John, the haughty antagonistic Red Comyn who was the rival of Robert Bruce, Earl of Carrick, the future king. At a time when a united nobility might have forced restraint on Edward I of England, the Bruce and Comyn factions divided the nation, playing most conveniently into his hands.

Not a single nobleman had come forward to offer direction to the people. When the extent of rebellion was realised, Robert Wishart, Bishop of Glasgow, and James the Steward renounced their allegiance to Edward and gave open support to the patriots. Both were to play a notable if sometimes dubious part in the fight for Scotland's independence.

The first knight to join Wallace was the fiery Sir William Douglas. Later in May 1297, they attacked the quarters of the justiciar, Sir William de Ormsby, at Scone. This hated official rounded on all who were reluctant to swear homage to Edward, imposing heavy fines and growing rich at the expense of those who resisted. He had warning of the approaching Scots and managed to escape – but only just, for he had to leave behind all his goods and belongings. When rumours of these affairs reached Edward he dispatched to Scotland Bishop Bek, who confirmed them, and on 12 July all Douglas's lands and estates in England were confiscated.

The Battle of Biggar, in which he has the Scots dispose of several thousands of the 60,000 English sent against them, is one of the Minstrel's most colourful engagements: 'fields planted with tents and pavilions, clarions blowing mighty sounds, provisions of wine and vitals brought down in carts'. Learned writers suggest that it is a duplicate of a later battle, there being no historical record of it from the English side. Prior to the fighting, two heralds went to Wallace's camp with a proclamation that if he surrendered to the King's peace, he should have pardon and reward. If he did not and was captured, he would hang. A kinsman of the King, a young squire named Fehew, wanting a sight of the Scottish chief, went in disguise with the heralds. He was recognised by Jop, and beheaded as a spy. The cruel mutilation of the two heralds Harry ascribes to Wallace. No such person as this 'Squir Fehew' can be traced, and the story is considered fabulous.[6] Even so, unless it be to his own advantage, Wallace was unlikely to deal leniently with any of the enemy who fell into his hands.

He was now in a formidable position, taking castles and restoring to Scotsmen their possessions. In Galloway only two strongholds held out against him – Wigton, and the castle of Cruggleton, on the River Cree. The first fell without a fight. The second, since it had been 'from time immemorable' the property of the Kerlies, calls for special attention. Built on a rock overhanging the bay, it was a massive place, and almost impregnable.

'That proportion of the precipice on which it stands juts out into the sea . . . the castle could never have been taken in flank, and the assault from the front, from the nature of the ground, must have been all but hopeless. A high battlemented wall swept round the courtyard . . . and the path from the precipice was seen and commanded, while a gate, fortified in the same manner (by a gatehouse, as at the harbour landing-place) defended the castle from surprise other side next the sea.'[7]

The manner of its capture, clearly detailed by the Minstrel, is considered dubious. 'The likelihood is' says Paterson, 'that the passage has not been correctly written.' Yet the lines that have puzzled earlier writers present no problem to the present-day reader. Positioning his small army out of sight, 'when the night was dim' Wallace took with him:

> 'Steven of Ireland, and Kerlie, that could clyme
> The wattir under; and clame the roch so strang;

Thus entrit thai the Southrone men among.'
*[Book VI, lines 816–818]*

Having scaled the rock below and above water, they reached the path and gate, the chief himself overpowering the porter and letting down the bridge. A blast on his horn brought his men out from the bushes below. They entered 'at will' and slew the garrison of sixty, sparing two women and one old priest. The castle was amply stocked, and there the Scots remained until its provisions were exhausted.

The most disturbing episode must surely be that often referred to as 'the famous story' of the Barns of Ayr – a description guaranteed to arouse scepticism. Yet the Minstrel speaks of it as 'well known'. Some 360 leading Scots were summoned by the new justice, Arnulf of Southampton, to attend an eyre[8] at Ayr on 18 June. Wondering at the purpose of such a council in time of peace, the sheriff, Sir Reginald Craufurd, first gathered his party at Monkton Church, where they were warned by the chaplain of mischief afoot. His suspicions were founded on the departure of Percy, who knew the peril that was to befall the Scots and had gone to Glasgow rather than be party to it. Wallace fell asleep in the church, where his cousin Kneland found him. In keeping with the times, the chroniclers allow the sleeper a wondrous vision, explained to him afterwards by a cleric.

Next day, riding to Ayr with his uncle, Wallace felt ill at ease. At Kingcase he enquired for the peace-bond drawn up earlier. It was in the charter-chest at Corsbie; nobody else would know where to find it, so, at his uncle's request, with three men Wallace rode back to collect the document, while the main party continued on its way. Arriving at the Barns to find the tollbooth guarded by 'stern men' the Scots were allowed to enter only one at a time, as they were called. By a noose slipped over the head they were hanged from a beam, Sir Reginald among the first. Wallace had been specially hoped for, but by this pure chance escaped the snare, to be informed on his return of the slaughter. Other knights on the Minstrel's list are Sir Bryce Blair, Sir Neil Montgomery, Campbells, Boyds, Barclays, Stewarts, and Kennedys.

Wallace's lieutenants, waiting for him in a tavern, were informed by a 'trew woman' of the massacre, of the bodies flung out, naked. Three hundred supporters quickly assembled in Laglane Woods.

From the five leaders one must be chosen: Boyd, Auchinlek, Adam Wallace (now Laird of Riccarton), William Craufurd (Sir Reginald's second son), or Wallace. Three times they cast for a leader and each time the lot fell to him. Drawing his sword, he vowed neither to eat nor drink till the deaths of his kinsmen and friends were avenged.

It was near to midsummer, yet on this fateful night only Scots appear to have been abroad. The 'trew woman', addressed by Wallace as 'der nece', Harry sends to chalk the doors where Englishmen lodged – an exercise that has a familiar ring to it! In the Barns, English soldiers celebrating on famous Irish ale were by night-time in a drunken stupor. They had set no guards, and they knew nothing of the incendiary preparations going on outside. The entire garrison was wiped out. Any who escaped the fire met the sword. So sickened by the outrage on their leading citizens were the friars that they themselves took arms and slew seven score of English billeted with them, an action known to Scots thereafter as 'The Blessing of the Friars of Ayr'.

The terrible and tragic prelude to the Burning of the Barns is often ignored, or treated as a 'minstrel's tale'. John Major, the fifteenth/sixteenth-century historian refers to it, as does a poem of 1548, *Complaynt of Scotland*. But it is to Barbour's *The Bruce* we must turn for evidence. An English knight, 'Crystoll of Seytoun', fought on the Scottish side. His grandson, Sir Christopher Seton, became the second husband of Christina Bruce, widow of the Earl of Mar. In 1306, Seton, then twenty-eight, was betrayed and captured. Barbour says he was taken to England; documents show, however, it was at Dumfries that he was hanged, drawn and quartered. Of his death the poet says:

'It wes gret sorrow sekyrly
That so worthy a persoune as he
Suld in sic maner hangyt be.
Thusgate endyt his worthiness.
**And of Crauford als Schyr Ranald wes;**
**And Schyr Bryce als the Blair**
**Hangyt in-till a berne at Ayr.'**[9]

The strongest argument against the hangings is the appearance at a later date of a Sir Reginald Craufurd. Documents confirm offices and gifts to Dougal MacDowall and others for the capture of the Bruce brothers, Thomas and Alexander, and *Sir Reginald Craufurd*, hanged at Carlisle on 17 February 1307. Craufurd's eldest son is rarely if ever taken into account: to maintain his birthright as hereditary Sheriff of Ayr, a young Sir Reginald must pay homage to King Edward, and could not openly support the patriots as his brother William did, and William is the second son. The execution in 1307 suggests a fall from grace of the young Sir Reginald when Edward's main preoccupation was the capture of Robert Bruce.

John Barbour, born about 1320, his boyhood spent under the zenith of King Robert's prestige, allows no detraction from his hero; the reader will search in vain for any mention of Wallace in his narrative. Why then should he bring into it such an irrelevancy as the hangings at Ayr in 1297 – nine years before the death of Seton – unless to protest against a deed he may well have learned of from his own father? If Harry's story is but an elaboration, as some claim, the bare facts remain in those three lines and the authority of Barbour.

Another eyre was called at Glasgow, under Bishop Bek and Percy – the more likely reason for the latter's departure. Expecting a similar atrocity, Wallace hastened to Glasgow. Harry tells of the good humour between him and Auchinlek, how they took each other by the hand before the latter, with Adam, attacked the English flank; while Wallace, with Boyd, pressed through the town, determined to 'bare the bishop's tail'. At Boswell, that war-like ecclesiastic came under the protection of Sir Aymer de Valence, Earl of Pembroke, cousin of King Edward.

About this time the suspicious behaviour of Bruce, Earl of Carrick, caused him to be summoned before the Bishop of Carlisle, when he swore on oath to 'lend faithful aid' to Edward against the Scots. As proof of his fidelity he attacked the estates of Sir William Douglas. Bruce and the King of England appear to be playing a despicable game, each using the other for his own ends with systematic selfishness. When his aspirations to the throne seemed threatened, Bruce transferred allegiance, and the King's accommodation of his behaviour fits the idea that he planned to put Bruce on the throne as his vassal. His father being in English custody, Carrick received little support from the men of Annandale, but with his own men, while in Edward's peace, embarked on a programme against him of wasting and slaying, the English clerics in particular receiving harsh treatment. With Wishart, Bishop of Glasgow, and James the Steward, he entered into a conspiracy, probably intending to seize the throne. But in July the armies of Percy and Clifford entered Annandale, Ayr, and Irvine, and any plot was doomed. The barons so disgusted one of their kind, Sir Richard de Lundin, that he openly transferred allegiance to Percy, though he had never before done homage to the English.

On 7 July 1297, the most powerful Scots nobles and their armies capitulated to Edward's commissioners at Irvine. In an 'ignominious document' they stated their fear that the King would press them into service overseas, and that they had taken up arms against him 'until they could protect themselves by treaty'. All were received into his peace, their lives and property guaranteed on the provision of hostages. Carrick was ordered to surrender his little daughter Marjorie – by his first and late wife, Isobel of Mar – but, say the historians, there is no evidence that he did so. Wishart and Douglas, unable or unwilling to provide hostages, were imprisoned in the castles of Roxburgh and Berwick respectively. Letters to Edward from the Treasurer, Cressingham, and one Spaldington, reported that Douglas, in irons, was 'still savage and abusive; I will keep him in such wise that please God, he shall by no means get out'. In October 1297 he was taken to the Tower, where, still in irons, he died in January 1298.

The barons' surrender at Irvine is said to have made Wallace extremely angry, in that it depleted his forces and undermined his leadership. But, according to ancient chroniclers, 'the whole *followers* of the nobility attached themselves to Wallace'. Cressingham, urged to raise money from the population to finance military operations against them, complained in a letter to Edward on 23 July, 'not a penny could be raised, but Sire, all will be speedily amended by the Grace of God and the return of the Earl of Warenne, Sir Henry Percy, Sir Robert Clifford, and others of your council, to compel the people by force of law'. The Treasurer also recommended an attack on William Wallace, then with a large company in Selkirk Forest, 'like one who holds himself against your peace'.

The King was anxious to embark for Flanders and, as usual, met 'almost insuperable difficulties' over men and money. The Jews, always a ready source, he expelled in 1290, and the Pope's writ, forbidding grants to laymen from church or clergy, was rigidly upheld by Robert Winchelsea, the new Archbishop of Canterbury.[10]

Edward tried other methods: from the sheriffs he demanded grain and cattle, and exorbitant taxes, without permission of parliament. All turned against him. Two of his great earls – Humphrey Bohun of Hereford, Constable of England, and Roger Bigod of Norfolk, the Marshal – stoutly resisted his demands – to the lasting benefit of the commons. Earlier in the year they refused to take armies to Gascony while he went to Flanders. Their high rank, they felt, entitled them to serve with their king. "By God, Sir Earl," cried Edward, "you shall either go or hang!" To which the Marshal replied, "Bigod, Sir King, shall neither go nor hang!" But this time, before he sailed for France on 22 August 1297, Edward had another card to play. Scottish knights captured at Dunbar the previous year were offered release if they would serve in France, their eldest sons to be held hostage meanwhile, all to be freed at the campaign's conclusion.

Sir Andrew Moray of Bothwell, held in the Tower of London, was unable to avail himself of this offer even if he would, for his son had escaped from Chester Castle. Making his way back to Moray, where his father's vassals were only too eager to rise against the English, young Andrew soon had in the field a formidable army. Castles were besieged and captured, lands burnt and laid waste, the enemy harassed or slain. Reports sent to Edward in July 1297 tell of 'a great body of rogues' and of the damage they were doing, as Moray moved his men southward.

Resting at Dundaff, Wallace received from Duncan MacDougall of Lorn, and Sir Neil Campbell of Lochow, an urgent request for assistance. Their lands, taken over by Edward, were given to and held down by the savagery of an Irishman named MacFadyan and a force of some 15,000, mostly Irish. John of Lorn, nicknamed 'Lame John', accepting an English lordship, gave up his heritage and left the fight to his younger brother. Wallace lost no time – he and Campbell had been school companions at Dundee. Earl Malcolm of Lennox, Sir Richard Lundin, Graham, Boyd, and Adam Wallace, with their supporters all joined the expedition to Argyllshire. Even with the Campbell and MacDougall men the Scots were numbered only in hundreds. But in the northern end of the Pass of Brandir they annihilated the enemy, setting up the head of MacFadyan on a rock. A council held afterwards at Ardchatten restored Argyll to Campbell, and all of Lorn to Duncan MacDougall, until such time as his brother should renounce allegiance to Edward and come home.

The two Highland chiefs would not forget the help so readily given by Lowland men.

Securing support on the way from the influential ecclesiastic, William Sinclair (later Bishop of Dunkeld), Wallace swept across country. 'By terror of his name' he reduced the castles and at Brechin displayed the Banner of Scotland. The important city of Aberdeen, set ablaze by the English, was still burning when the Scots entered, to plunder and set on fire enemy supply ships in the harbour. Andrew de Moray was close by; the first meeting of the two commanders is thought to have taken place about this time. At Dunnattor hundreds of English took refuge in a church. All perished when Wallace, despite entreaties from Sinclair, ordered the building to be fired. Fresh on his mind, says the Minstrel, was the atrocity at Ayr.

Most of the country north of the Forth was now under his control. Dundee and Stirling were the next important objectives. During the siege of the former, Wallace received reports of English army movements, and leaving 2,000 men there under one of his lieutenants – possibly Scrymgeour – he led his main army towards Stirling, there to be reinforced by Moray's successful contingents. The pitched battle Wallace had so far managed to avoid was upon him, though on a site of his own choosing. With their backs to the Abbey Craig, the Ochills behind, the looping Forth at their front, the Scots took up positions and settled down to await the arrival of the English. Earl Warenne was ill, and perhaps a little out of favour. He had been replaced as Governor by Sir Brian Fitz Alan and was anxious to be relieved of his military duties also. But orders were that he remain at his post. Marching from Berwick, his forces reached Stirling on 10 September.

The Scots up to now had experienced only guerilla warfare, their weapons pikes and spears. There had been no war for nearly a century and few, if any, knew military training or military discipline. Their leaders certainly did not. Yet here at Stirling they displayed with 'instinctive military genius' a strategy that even the enemy could not fail to admire. In the morning the two armies lay in full view of each other and the English commander, noting the advantageous position of the Scots, allowed the Earl of Lennox and James the Steward – then on the English side – to send over two friars. Wallace, on being invited to enter the King's peace replied, "Take back for answer that we are not here to sue for peace, but we are ready to fight for the freedom of our country and ourselves. Let the English come on when they please; they will find us ready to meet them to their beards." The friars estimated Scottish strength to be 180 horse and 40,000 foot. The Treasurer, Cressingham, stingy as ever over matters of finance, dismissed Percy's force of 8,000 foot and 300 horse. Warenne's strength was 1,000 horse and 50,000 foot[11] – more than enough to contain the Scots.

Between the armies was a swampy boggy carse. If Warenne expected Wallace to relinquish his higher sheltered ground and meet him on the broad plain, he seriously underestimated his man. While the commander hesitated, Cressingham grew more impatient at the waste of time and the King's money. The only way across the Forth was by a wooden bridge, wide enough to take two horses abreast. Sir Richard Lundin, the baron who defected earlier, knew of a ford where sixty could cross at a time. He offered to lead a party across, to engage the Scots while the main body crossed over the bridge. Lundin knew the ground – and he knew Wallace – but his offer was rejected. Warenne, unwell, allowed himself to be persuaded by Cressingham, and that detested churchman, on the morning of 11 September 1297, led across the narrow bridge of Stirling the ponderous warhorses with their heavily armed knights, the spearmen and the Welsh archers. From the highest point of the Abbey Craig Wallace watched and waited, his forces held in admirable restraint. At eleven o'clock he gave the signal, a blast on his horn, and from the wooded slopes his troops poured down, encircling the enemy and seizing the bridgehead. In the dreadful melee that followed, Cressingham paid quickly for his impulsiveness, Warenne watching helplessly as his army was cut to pieces by compact bodies of Scottish spearmen. Horses, carriages and troops, jam-packed on the bridge and unable to turn back, were hampered by others in retreat. The frightful press spilled over into the Forth where mailed knights and chargers quickly drowned or were carried away on the tidal waters. The yet unformed ranks of foot, thrown into confusion, were slaughtered on the field or driven into the river to a watery end. Earl Warenne, seeing the battle lost, rode away with his entourage as fast as their horses would carry them, his own exhausted to its death. The Earl of Lennox and James the Steward bringing up extra horse, now joined the winning side in pursuit of the English to the Border.

The body of Cressingham is said to have been flayed and the

skin cut into strips for use as sword-belts, saddle girths and other exaggerated notions, all recorded and repeated by enemies of Wallace, implying that such behaviour was a peculiarity of his. The English chronicler, Hemingburgh, who might be expected to make much of this, reports simply that 'the skin was cut into strips, not as relics, but for hatred of him'. It was perhaps fortunate for Cressingham that he was slain in battle and died honourably, for he was hated by both sides equally. He had at times withheld the English soldiers' pay and was in danger of being stoned to death by them before the battle for dismissing Percy's force.

The Minstrel's story of the bridge – which Lord Hailes considers 'too childish to repeat' yet does – is that Wallace caused it to be sawn through, the cut disguised with clay and the carpenter, 'Jhon the Wricht'[12], slung underneath in a cradle. A beam or 'pyn', previously loosened, was to be withdrawn at a given signal, causing the structure to collapse at the strategic moment. As Harry tells it, the chief marvels at his own ingenuity! If there is any truth in the tale it does not seem applicable either to the bridge or battle at Stirling.[13]

First, there is the story of Sir Marmaduke de Twenge. Commanding a body of mounted knights he was among the first English to cross and on his way uphill to engage the Scottish cavalry at the time Wallace's foot-troops seized the bridgehead. Realising that his men could be trapped, and refusing to throw himself into the river where he would surely drown, de Twenge ordered his men to turn, to follow him closely and he would cut a path back. With flailing sword and utmost valour, and bearing a wounded comrade, he *regained the bridge and crossed it*, earning the respect of both sides. The gallant Englishman was imprisoned in Dumbarton Castle, according to some reports without the customary irons.

The second consideration is the bridge itself. The weakened structure nevertheless withstood the passage of half the English force. The weight on the bridge at the time would have rendered the withdrawal of the 'pyn' a remarkable feat, and surely a suicidal one for the workman, could he have accomplished it.

Thirdly, Wallace is said never to have allowed the enemy any opportunity of gaining advantage over him, and he had learned also never to waste a single good man. It seems unlikely that he cut the path of pursuit. The destruction of the bridge after the battle, to prevent the English re-forming and turning the tables on the Scots, is the more credible explanation. Wallace himself crossed at the ford referred to by Lundin.

The two commanders were at once the most important men in the land – the nation's heroes. At a council summoned by the Community – that is, the sheriffs, burgesses and other dignitaries – they were elected Generals of the Army in the name of King John, though Moray suffered injuries at the bridge that were soon to prove fatal. Attempts are made here and there to deprive Wallace of his great victory, to make him the subordinate of Moray. Andrew, like William, was the son of a knight, though a much more influential one, heir to vast estates and, as we have seen, with a large number of vassals to call upon. Wallace neither owned nor was heir to any family wealth; his elder brother had the heritage. Younger sons had to make and earn a living, and until the invasion of Scotland William was still at his studies, possibly with a view to entering the church – a calling he intended to pursue once his purpose was achieved:

'For as of war he was in sumpart irk;
He purposed then to serve God and the Kirk'.
*[Book XII, lines 961–962]*

and to live 'in lasting peace with his rightwise king'. So says the Minstrel. If William's circumstances serve to enhance his courage, those of Andrew diminish his not one jot. But at Stirling it is Wallace's reply to the friars that is recorded, *he* who from the Craig gave the signal for battle:

'In all that host no one should blaw but he.'
*[Book VII, line 1162]*

Is it likely, had Moray planned the battle, had the strategy been his, that he would have relinquished it to Wallace's undoubted command? With respect to the memory of the equally brave young Andrew and his dauntless comrades, it is clearly under William Wallace that the deliverance of Scotland was achieved.

Writings found in monasteries say that after the victory Wallace returned to the interrupted siege of Dundee. 'If this is true,' says Fergusson, 'it is evidence of a highly practical mind refusing to be deflected . . . from completing a task already begun.'[14] That castle quickly fell, Stirling shortly after, yielding valuable supplies and booty to the Scots. In ten days the only English left in Scotland were the prisoners.

By an extraordinary and quite irresistible coincidence, there is a connection between this period of history and the writer's home village in Norfolk. John de Warenne, 6th Earl of Surrey and one of the most powerful men of his day, belonged, like King Edward, to the great Angevin family known as Plantagenet. In reply to Edward's writ of 1278, *Quo Warranto*, Warenne unsheathed his rusty sword: "Here, sirs, is my warrant. My ancestors came over with William the Bastard and won their lands by the sword, and by the sword I mean to keep them." His wife Alice was half-sister of Henry III. 'Grandees of the first magnitude,' the family owned hundreds of properties – one, a manor and house at the settlement of Methelwold in Norfolk. To this place, because of his failing health, the Earl probably retired after his defeat by William Wallace, his only son William having been killed in a tournament at Croydon.

A vicar of Methwold (1873–1902) writes that from non-residence the property fell into decay, that its stones may have been used in building the church of St George on the elevation above it, splendidly sited and a magnificent landmark. 'From the tower at sundown foundations of Warenne's palace are traceable' says the vicar, and he gives a conjectural rendering of the east frontage. (See *The Life of a Village Community in the Eastern Counties* by Rev. J. Denny Gedge, Vicar of Methwold, 1893.)

Blomefield's *Norfolk,* 1738, vol. ii, from p. 202, however, raises the church in the reign of Edward II (1307–1327), before the property at Methelwold was willed by the Warennes to the Earldom of Lancaster in 1347. This became a Dukedom on 6 March 1351, when Edward III made his fourth son, John of Gaunt, its first Duke through marriage to Blanche, great-granddaughter of Edmund (Crouchback) Earl of Lancaster, brother of Edward I.

If the outer buildings had fallen into decay, the manor house itself appears to have survived and to have been of some importance in 1381. In the Peasants' Uprising in East Anglia it was attacked and the court roll destroyed on 16 June of that year. (See *The Rising in East Anglia in 1381* by Edgar Powell BA, 1896, p. 27.)

The Warenne site has beyond living memory been the village recreation ground, unsatisfactory as such because of the stones. Cleared and levelled after the Second World War – when bombs fell, missing the church by yards – it is now a valued amenity.

# Chapter VII

Scotland was free, but the country in too lamentable a state for much rejoicing. Wallace received all who would swear 'a great oath' to himself and to Scotland. Amongst those who came was Sir John Stewart of Menteith, a relative of the High Steward. Another noble, loyal throughout to King Edward, refused to take the oath. Wallace would not at first proceed against him. But at a second invitation the black-bearded Corspatrick, Earl of Dunbar, sent back an insulting reply to the 'king of Kyle'. Whether this was a derisory reference to the prominence of the Wallaces in Kyle, or to William's life as an outlaw in the forests, is open to argument still. Wallace sought out and defeated the Earl, who fled across the Border.

While King Edward remained in France there would be a brief respite, his return the signal for a fresh invasion to avenge defeat at Stirling. By dividing the country into military districts, with a roll of all men between the ages of sixteen and sixty capable of carrying arms, Wallace set about the task of restoring order and discipline. His method was remarkable: over every fourth man he placed a fifth; over every ninth a tenth; over every nineteenth a twentieth, graduating to the thousand. In each parish a gibbet was erected, with not a few hangings 'to enforce respect'. Barons were threatened with imprisonment or confiscation of property if they prevented any of their vassals who wished from joining the army. The common people were near to starvation – crops had been burned and their homes destroyed. The happy discovery by Dr Lappenberg in Lubeck in 1829 of a document still extant shows that in a matter of weeks the two generals were seeking to re-establish trade abroad:

*'Andrew de Moray and William Wallace, commanders of the army of the kingdom of Scotland, and the community of the*

*same kingdom – To the prudent and discreet men, and well-beloved friends, the Mayors of Lubeck and of Hamburg, greeting, and perpetual increase of sincere friendship.*

*'To us it has been intimated by trustworthy merchants of the said kingdom of Scotland, that, as a mark of your regard, you have been favourable to, counselling and assisting in all matters and transactions relating to us and said merchants, though [such good offices] may not have been preceded by our deserts, and on that account we are the more bound to tender you our thanks, and a suitable return. This we have willingly engaged ourselves to [perform towards] you, requesting, that in so far you would cause your merchants to be informed that they will now have safe access to all the ports of the kingdom of Scotland with their merchandise, as the kingdom of Scotland, thanks to God, has during the war been recovered from the power of the English. Farewell. – Given at Haddington, in Scotland, this eleventh day of October, in the year of grace, one thousand two hundred and ninety-seven. – We have, moreover, to request that you would condescend to forward the interests of our merchants, John Burnet and John Frere, in their business, in like manner as you may wish us to act towards your merchants in their commercial transactions. Farewell.'*

William Fraser, Primate, and Bishop of St Andrews, the writer in 1290 of the letter to King Edward, died in 1297. The English chose William Comyn, brother of the Earl of Buchan, to replace him. Wallace persuaded the canons of St Andrews to appoint instead William Lamberton, Chancellor of Glasgow and a known patriot. He was consecrated by Pope Boniface VIII in Rome in 1298.

To alleviate the calamities of famine and plague Wallace prepared to march an army into England, 'that they might acquire health and strength by the exercise',[1] thus sparing such provisions as there were for the people at home. No great lord who if captured could be held for ransom was to accompany the expedition – a further example of the commander's prudence. Twenty thousand seasoned men were selected; as many more he put to the task of reconstruction and the restoration of the land. Earl Malcolm, Campbell of Lochow, Graham, Boyd, Auchinlek, Ramsey, Hay, Seton, Lauder, and Lundin[2] were among the leaders who crossed with him into England on 31 October 1297.

Warned of the Scottish army's approach, inhabitants of the northern counties fled south, taking with them such treasure, goods and cattle as could be moved. For the sufferings inflicted on their own country the invaders exerted a merciless revenge: lands were burnt and wasted, the people robbed and slain. 'The praise of God ceased' says Hemingburgh, 'in all monasteries and churches from Newcastle-upon-Tyne to Carlisle.' (As it would if all the priests had fled!) Alnwick Castle in Northumberland, home of the Percys, like Carlisle heavily fortified, the Scots made no attempt to capture. But from an English baron, Sir Robert de Ros of Wark, they received actual assistance in wasting the countryside around.

Harry sends Wallace and his army on to York and even to St Albans! He tells of the English refusing battle unless Wallace assumed the crown. His supporters – Campbell, in particular – were insistent that he should do so. After much deliberation among the leaders, and soul-searching by Wallace, he reluctantly agreed to the suggestion of Earl Malcolm, and on Northallerton Moor took the crown for a day, in order to draw the English into battle. 'As mine auctor will say,' asserts Harry. Towards the end of his narrative he records that two knights, 'Wallas and Liddaill', got him to say otherwise then 'Maister Blayr', whose account 'we did sumpart off dispys'.

At St Albans Harry has the Scottish army camped 'for some time'; even with Edward abroad this must be rejected. Yet it cannot be beyond the bounds of possibility that a small band of determined men reached Hertfordshire, where they believed their king to be, unaware that with the patriotic uprisings John Baliol had been secretly moved to the Tower of London.[3]

A queen's involvement is another matter: there was no Queen of England from 1290–1299, when Edward married again. But early in 1298, still in France and desperately short of money, his council was anxious to establish peace at home. Because of the fierce reputation of the Scottish Chief no one could be found to approach him.

The Queen, so the story goes, undertakes to act as messenger. With fifty ladies, seven aged priests, gifts of gold and delicacies, she rides to Wallace's camp at St Albans and makes for the pavilion where flies the Lion of Scotland, to be greeted by Earl Malcolm. The Chief, though in ignorance of the visit, had fortunately put on full armour, all shining and clean, sword in hand and Jop in attendance. With Adam Wallace and Boyd, walking by a river and enjoying the beauty of an English morning, he watches the Queen's party ride by, and returns to camp to welcome her. At dinner she samples first the dishes she has brought, that Wallace might be assured there was no attempt to poison him. She listens with sympathy and understanding to the grievous wrongs that have befallen his family and country, the reasons for his subsequent actions against the English.

The Queen was thought by some to be in love with Wallace. (Harry will say nothing; he cannot believe she would take on such a task for love; he is only reporting the rumour.) Yet for all her womanly charms and offers of gold, she could not move him from his resolve. Neither would he conclude with a woman a treaty that could later be declared void, and used as an excuse for further treachery. All that was achieved was an assurance of protection for any of Edward's envoys on errands of peace.

There can be no basis at all for this story in the spring or early summer of 1298. Margaret of France, Edward's second wife, had not then entered the arena of British history. The 'romantic nonsense' may be resigned to the pages of Miss Porter's excruciating yet engrossing novel.[4]

More reliable is the report of a proposed attack on Durham and its warrior bishop, when the Scots were hampered by a terrible snowstorm in which many perished. This 'intervention' by St Cuthbert, the guardian saint, as well as exaggerated reports of Bek's military strength, dissuaded Wallace from further penetration into England and he turned his army back.

To Hexham Priory in Northumberland, left in ruins by the Earl of Buchan in March 1296, three canons had returned and built an oratory. Now these returning soldiers bursting in, demanding their treasure or their lives, were reminded by one canon, "Your people carried off our treasure, and you know best what they have done with it. We have but a few things, as you see." Wallace entered and ordered his men to withdraw. Asking the canon to celebrate mass, he went to lay aside his sword. In his absence the soldiers again crowded round the canon, snatching the chalice and vestments, even the book he was using. Returning to find him frightened and alone, Wallace gave orders for the culprits to be found and beheaded. But they were not, because, says Hemingburgh, 'the seeking was without intention of finding'. The canons Wallace took under his personal protection, advising that they stay close to him, as his men were 'full of mischief.' He issued two charters, of protection and safe conduct. These are preserved in full by the contemporary English chronicler and translated by later ones:

*'Andrew de Moray and William Wallace, Generals of the army of Scotland, in the name of the renowned Prince Lord John, by the grace of God, the illustrious King of Scotland, with the consent of the said realm, to all men of the said realm to whom the present writing shall come, greeting.*

*'Know that we, in the name of the said King, have duly taken the Prior and convent of Hexham in Northumberland, their lands, their men and their possessions, including all their goods, movable and immovable, under the firm peace of the said King and ourselves. Wherefore we strictly forbid that any person do them evil, annoyance, injury, or offence to their persons, lands or goods, under penalty or forfeiture of all the offender's property to the said King; or to put them, or any one of them, to death, under penalty of loss of life and limbs. These presents to remain in force for one year and no longer.*

*'Given at Hexham, November 7.'*

Murison p. 95

The letter of safe conduct, similarly constructed, enables the canon, his squire and two attendants 'to come to us wherever we may be'. The charters make no mention of knighthood, as they surely would had it then been a fact. But the placing of Moray's name before that of Wallace again gives rise to the supposition that Wallace was the junior in command, and that both were actively involved in the invasion of England. There is often confusion over the three generations of Morays relevant to this period. Sir Andrew de Moray, Lord of Bothwell, held prisoner in the Tower since the Battle of Dunbar in April 1296, is unlikely to have been a supporter of Wallace before that date. His son Andrew, as we have seen, escaped and led the uprising in Morayshire in 1297. Wounded at Stirling in September, dead in November, it is highly improbable that he accompanied Wallace into England in October. Neither could his son have done so. The report of an inquisition at Berwick in 1300 mentions that the child was then 'two years of age and living in Moray among the king's enemies.'[5] Buchanan, at least, is decisive;

of the Battle of Stirling Bridge he writes, 'This victory, in which no Scottish man of any distinction fell, except Andrew de Moray, whose son,[6] some years after, was regent of Scotland, was gained in 13th September 1297.'[7] Under the circumstances, the joint command of Moray and Wallace appears as a formality only. Murison suggests that 'baronial considerations may explain official precedence of Moray's name'[8], to placate the nobles who resented Wallace. An earlier biographer, John D. Carrick, writing in 1830, concludes that the letter to the Mayors was either written by Wallace or at his dictation, and considers it 'quite in keeping with the amiableness and modesty of his character' that he should have placed Moray's name before his own. 'Had it been written or dictated by Moray, he would probably have exercised the same courtesy, by placing the name of Wallace first. It is as probable, however, that he placed Moray's name first to show that he was not actuated by motives of ambition.'[9]

Medieval knights enjoyed the privilege of dubbing others, especially for valour and distinguished service in battle. Wallace certainly qualified and authoritative writers do not doubt the honour, only the timing is in question and by whose hand bestowed. The Earls of Lennox and Carrick are possible candidates during one of Bruce's phases of sympathy with his countrymen. Wyntoun's statement, that Wallace 'Come after the Yule into Scotland' gives him two months over the Border, and writers some room for manipulation.

While the Scots were in England Sir Robert de Clifford marched an army into their country, to pillage and burn, but he too retired about Christmas time. Wallace toured Scotland, settling the land and the people. His loyal lieutenants he rewarded with positions of authority, but for himself and his family he took nothing, being prepared to wait for such rewards as his lawful king on his return should judge him worthy.

Preparations began in England for a renewed attack on Scotland. With the King still in France, Warenne, again in military command, went to consult the thirteen-year-old Prince of Wales at York, and in January marshalled at Newcastle a massive force. Before leaving England in August, King Edward tearfully admitted his wrongdoing over taxes, and promised an assembly at Westminster Hall that wool, grain, cattle, and other commodities would in due course be paid for. In November, amendments to Magna Carta and the Charter of the Forests were taken to him at Ghent, where he put his seal to the document *Confirmatio Chartarum*, renouncing the right of taxing the people without consent of parliament. The pacified barons turned out in strength to a parliament at York on 14 January 1298.

Edward, meanwhile, was concluding terms of peace with France. He sent directions that Warenne should hold Berwick but make no further advances until his arrival. Disbanding part of his army, the luckless commander was left still with 1,500 armed horse and 20,000 foot. The 'bloodless victory' at Stanmore in Cumberland, when raw and hastily levied troops are said to have retreated rather than risk battle against Scottish veterans,[10] is obscure, involving Wallace, as it would, in a second invasion of England. But there must have been something to stir and increase the jealousy of his enemies at home. That he obtained the title and position of Guardian is placed beyond doubt by an extant charter granting to Alexander Scrymgeour the standard-bearer the hereditary Constableship of Dundee, an office held ever since by Scrymgeour's descendants.

*'Sir William Wallace, Guardian of Scotland, in the name of King John Baliol, with the seal of the said John . . . by the consent and approbation of the grandees of the said kingdom, give and concede to Alexander Skirmscher six merks of land in the territory of Dundee . . . also the Constabulary of the Castle of Dundee . . . for the faithful service and assistance rendered to this aforesaid kingdom, in bearing the royal standard in the army of Scotland, at the time the present writing has been drawn up. In the testimony of which the common seal of the aforesaid kingdom of Scotland has been affixed to the present writing.*

*'Given at Torphichen 29th day of March in the year of grace 1298.'*

Paterson p.198; Murison p.99

The wording of the charter, the common seal and that of King John, all give credence to the popular belief that Wallace was *elected* Guardian in the Forest of Selkirk, receiving the accolade at the same ceremony.

Some of the nobles looked favourably on King Edward; some who did not he kept in his grip by holding their relatives hostage. Who among them would dare to stand against him and the might of England? Only Wallace, the common people solidly behind him, had nothing left to lose but his life. Scottish nobles summoned to the parliament at York on 14 January 'neither came nor sent'. This is at least suggestive that he was then firmly established in supreme power. To have styled himself 'Guardian' or to have assumed the position without authority or consent would be in complete contrast to almost every estimate of his character.

"From this period" says Lord Hailes, "I presume to date that jealousy which the great barons of Scotland entertained of Wallace."[11] Rumours spread that he was aspiring to the throne. Yet he acted always in the name of King John, constitutionally upholding the lawful ruler. In this he might have expected support from Sir John Comyn, Lord of Badenoch and Baliol's nephew. But for the 'base-born' son of a small laird, the Red Comyn cherished a bitter envy. To his rival Robert Bruce he displayed a cold contemptuous dislike – a state of affairs not unknown to King Edward.

The Guardian stayed for a while with Sir John Stewart of Menteith, Constable of Dumbarton, and there set up his own house. It must have been during this period that he stood godfather to two of Menteith's children. In the words of the Minstrel – which the historian John Major supports:

'Twyss befor he had his gossep beyn
But na frendchip betwixt them since was seyn.'
*[Book VIII, lines 1597–1598]*

At Roxburgh, on a site specially chosen, a tower was built for Sir William:

'Was nayn so gret durst his nychtbour displess.'
*[Book VIII, line 1606]*

The scene depicted by Harry, of labourers at work, the 'able ground' producing an abundance of 'froyte and vitals' during five months of peace, conceivable further north, is barely so in an area of such devastation. With Warenne's bored and disgruntled troops kicking their heels in the Border towns, encounters between the two sides would be numerous and bloody.

# Chapter VIII

King Edward returned to England on 14 March 1298, landing at Sandwich, and at once set in motion his plans for the Scottish expedition. He proceeded to York and, while his armies were gathering, held a parliament. For the second time Scottish nobles 'neither came nor sent'. Edward made a pilgrimage to the shrine of St John of Beverley before progressing to Roxburgh. From there he led the army to Kirkliston where he camped to await supplies.

Sir Aymer de Valence and Sir John Siward with their armies sailed direct from France, landing in Fife. On 12 June they were heavily defeated by the Scots at Blackearnside. In a respite from fighting, Wallace carried water in a helmet from a nearby stream to his wounded men, instead of taking a much needed rest. In the heat of the day, remarks Harry:

> 'The wine of France he thought not half so good!'
>
> *[Book X, line 284]*

Sir John Graham and one of the Setons were among the wounded this day.

Additional English forces crossed the Tweed on 3 July. Unfavourable winds delayed the arrival at Berwick of the provision fleet, and for a fortnight Wallace besieged Carlisle Castle so that desperately needed supplies could be brought neither in nor out. Land convoys too were attacked by Scottish raiding parties, and Bishop Bek was sent to destroy the three castles from which they were operating. Failing in his task, he sent to the King a messenger, Sir John Fitz Marmaduke, for instruction. Edward's reply, according to Hemingburgh, is as follows:

"Go back and tell the bishop that in so far as he is a bishop he is a good man, but that his goodness is out of place for this task. You are a relentless soldier, Marmaduke. I have often had to reprove you for too cruel exultation over the death of your enemies. But return whence you came, and be as relentless as you choose – you will deserve my thanks, not my censure. But look you do not see my face again till these three castles are razed to the ground."

As soon they were!

Edward's soldiers, hungry, dispirited and inactive, began to fight among themselves. Two hundred casks of wine arrived which he ordered to be distributed freely. The Welsh archers got drunk and attacked the English, who killed eighty of them, and for their efforts at peacemaking eighteen priests also died. On being told of the possibility of the Welsh going over to the Scots the King replied, "What matter if enemies join with enemies? Let them go where they please."

Wallace meanwhile, harassing the enemy at every opportunity, kept his main army out of sight in the vastness of the forests. The further inland he could draw the English the more desperate would be their plight in retreat. With the area for miles around cleared of cattle, no sustenance from the scorched and barren land for either men or horses, Edward at last gave orders for the retreat to Edinburgh. Two Scottish earls consistently loyal to him, March and Angus – said by Hemingburgh to have spied on the Scots positions – in league with Bishop Bek, early on 21 July sent a boy to the King to report Wallace camped in the Forest of Selkirk, near Falkirk. This intelligence delighted Edward; he suddenly reversed the order to retire and at once prepared to march. Near Linlithgow the army rested, and in readiness for an early move all were to sleep beside their horses. An inattentive groom allowed Edward's great charger to step on the King during the night, breaking two ribs. Rumour spread through the camp that the Scots had attacked and uproar ensued. Great warrior that he was, Edward in spite of his pain mounted another horse and, moving among his men, restored confidence. Before dawn on 22 July, the mighty English army, said to number 100,000, passed Linlithgow towards Falkirk. In the light of day the Scottish army could be seen on the sloping plain, drawn up for battle.

Against odds of three to one, Wallace would not have sought or welcomed pitched battle; undoubtedly the English reversal upset his plan. Yet if by strategy he had reduced the enemy to the point of retreat, it is extremely unlikely that he was caught out by the sudden change. Under new circumstances, he pursued what seemed to him the wisest and most honourable course. The King moved his great army on one day; Wallace could have done the same with his lesser one, and retired to the more favourable ground of Stirling and the natural protections afforded there. But the risk was too great; Edward's cavalry would have hacked the retreating Scots to pieces. Face to face with the ageing King of England and his starving mutinous army, the Guardian of Scotland would make his stand.

His infantry, thought to number 30,000, Wallace placed in 'schiltrons', circular bodies of spearmen at least three ranks deep, the front line kneeling, each rank rising above the other. Shoulder to shoulder, their twelve-foot spears slanting out over the heads of the men in front presented to the enemy a 'forest of steel'. If not the originator of the 'bristling hedgehog' form of defence, Wallace may be seen as its perfecter. Within the circles other spearmen stood, to replace any who fell. In front of the positions lay a peat bog, stuck with long stakes connected by ropes to form a stockade, to trap or impede the English cavalry. Between the four great schiltrons were bodies of archers, led by Sir John Stewart of Bonkil, and to the rear the cavalry, 1,000 strong, was under the command of Sir John Comyn. Other prominent leaders included Macduff, great-uncle of the young Earl of Fife; Sir John Graham; Robert Boyd; Sir Henry de Haliburton; and Sir Nichol de Rutherford. Before the battle Wallace addressed his troops: "I haf brocht ye ta the ring; hop [dance] if ye can." Recorded by the contemporary chronicler, Matthew of Westminster, it is believed to be the only authentic saying of Wallace. For some it is heavy with despair; for others it glows with the excitement of battle, with confidence in his men and in his own leadership.

But mischievous forces were at work. Comyn and Stewart became embroiled in 'heated dissension' over the leadership. Comyn sought to persuade the brother of the High Steward that pride of place was rightly his. Wallace, Harry says, 'burnt as fire' at this insolence. He saw the design and well knew the instigator, though Comyn left the hurling of insults to the other. If their own kind were there, said Stewart, Wallace would have but few supporters. He was like an owl decked out in finer feathers. Reminding him that he had twice rescued Comyn from danger, and had ventured where Stewart dare not show his face, the Guardian warned that for his arrogance he could die, or bide in prison, and further:

> '"Reskew off me thow shall get none this day."'
> *[Book XI, line 157]*

Stewart is said to have regretted his part, but further argument was silenced by the advancing English cavalry under the Earl Marshal and the Earls of Hereford and Lincoln, with the second division under Bishop Bek and Sir Ralph Basset. Infantry and archers the King commanded in person. Into the bog went the first charge, the Earl Marshal extricating himself and his men to strike at the right of the schiltrons. Witnessing the embarrassment, Bek skirted the bog and led his division round to strike at the left, quickly disposing between them of the hedge of stakes. But the brave resolute spearmen of the schiltrons could not be broken or ridden down: 'As a castelle they stood, that was walled with stone,' writes the English canon, Peter Langtoft. Edward was getting nowhere and losing fine horses on Scottish steel. His cavalry turned their attention to the Scots archers. Within the schiltrons these would have been unassailable, though restricted in range. Outside them they were defenceless against armed assault and gave way. Macduff and his Fife men went down; Sir John Stewart, unhorsed and fighting on foot, died where he stood, his 'fine tall men' bravely forming about him. And still the schiltrons held, as they would later do at Flodden:

> 'The stubborn spearmen still made good
> Their dark impenetrable wood
> Each stepping where his comrade stood
> The instant that he fell.'

Edward ordered the archers to attack but they would not move. Since his conquest of Wales they bore him only hatred, though for payment were willing to fight in his wars. He brought forward the infantry to hurl stones and missiles, and the archers, perceiving a turning point in the battle, then launched a hail of arrows from their deadly longbows, and the front line of the schiltrons was broken. Seeing the English armed horse thundering in for the kill, the Scots cavalry under Comyn turned and fled from the field without ever being engaged or striking a single blow in the conflict. Wallace, his horse shot from under him, joined his foot-troops in the thick of the fighting where he could wield his great sword to best effect. 'Like snow in winter' his men fell, 'upwards of ten thousand' dead and dying men and horses trampled into a gory morass by the living. On the English side 'the only person of note to fall' was Sir Brian Jay, Master of the Templars.

The behaviour of Sir John Comyn at Falkirk has all the appearance of treachery and desertion. Yet the cap of cowardice does not fit him or his men, and he had never gone over to Edward. But another victory for Wallace and the wave of public acclaim could push that man towards the throne. Without the support of 1,000 cavalry his chances of victory were lessened, and, even if he survived the battle, defeat would turn the people against him. If this was the Red Comyn's scheme, it succeeded, though perhaps not quite in the way hoped for. 'We should be glad' says Murison, 'to discover some less dastardly reason for his ignominious conduct at Falkirk.'[1] Only one other motive presents itself: his wife, Johanna de Valence, sister of Sir Aymer and cousin of Edward, was ordered to London with her children in March 1298 – if the date is reliable, about the time of the King's return from France. But Wallace was then at the height of his power, the virtual dictator of Scotland. It is incomprehensible that he would allow valuable hostages to be delivered into English custody, or that Sir John would bow to such an order at this time.

Where was Robert Bruce on this fateful day? Was he 'holding Ayr' fifty miles away as Lord Hailes and Mr Barron insist?[2] Ancient Scots chroniclers, on the other hand, are 'almost unanimous' in asserting his presence at Falkirk under Bishop Bek, and stating that he was responsible for breaking the schiltrons from the rear. A point of view in Moir's notes is certainly persuasive:

'It is [not] likely that men like Wyntoun and Fordun, writing after Bruce had made himself a revered and beloved monarch . . . would have ventured to say [this] unless it had been the account universally received in Scotland.'[3]

The remaining Scots army drew off towards Stirling. Wounded and exhausted, yet reluctant to leave his fallen comrades, Wallace was led from the field, and with Kerlie he rested on the banks of the Carron.

Bruce with his company approached the opposite bank and called across that he desired a conference. Wallace agreed; though he would have little to say, he was curious to hear what the Earl of Carrick could have to say to him! Without attendants 'where the river narrows' the two men faced each other. What was his purpose, Bruce asked, in exposing himself to constant danger, when he could live as a lord in Edward's peace? He could expect no reward, and even if he conquered Edward, the Scots would never allow him to reign. Wallace replied, so Harry says, that he claimed no right; it was neither his desire nor his purpose to seize the crown; such a charge was not to be borne. The inactivity of the nobles, indeed, the treachery of Bruce, who should rightly be king yet had turned on his own countrymen, had caused him to pity the people so oppressed and, since God had given him might, he had taken up their cause – one he would never forsake. Was not Bruce ashamed that *he* had never yet done good? In any field, Wallace vowed to God, "may I your master be".

Night was approaching and Bruce requested further consultation at the chapel of Dunipace 'at nine of bell' in the morning. Still not trusting, Wallace preferred an earlier meeting: he would be there 'at the hour of three'. Bruce promised to come with twelve men and Wallace gave assurance, come they as friend or foe, they would meet with no force from his ten. The two then went their separate ways.

King Edward returned to Linlithgow to rest and to repair his broken ribs. To the camp Bruce rode and, in the royal pavilion where supper was set, Harry puts into his mouth his famous line:

'So entryt in, and saw vacand hys seit.
No watter he tuk, bot maid hym to the meit.
Fastand he was, and had beyne in gret dreid;
Bludyt was in all hys wapynes and hys weid.
Sotheron lordis scornyt him in termis rud
And said, "Behold, yon Scot ettes hys owyn blud!"
The king thocht ill thai maid sic derision;
He bad watter to Bruce off Huntytoun.
Thai bad hym wesche; he said that wald be nocht;
**"This blud is myn, that hurtis most my thocht."'**
*[Book XI, lines 531–540]*

Filled with remorse, Bruce pondered over the reasoning of Wallace and knew it to be right; had he behaved differently the lifeblood and land of Scotland should all have been his own. Throughout his life and long before, family ambition was directed towards the crown.

The patriotic cause, in the name of King John, was therefore in direct opposition to his. But the exiled and imprisoned king had renounced his right. Then along comes the upstart Wallace, seemingly with aspirations of his own. How could Bruce support either? He was not the head of the family, his father was still alive and in England. Such was the dilemma of Robert Bruce during the first chapter of the war of independence.

There was little sleep this summer night. Wallace assembled a host of 5,000 and returned to the battlefield. In his own party are named Earl Malcolm, Ramsey, Lundin, Lauder, Seton, and Adam Wallace. When they found the body of Sir John Graham, the Guardian alighted and gathered up the corpse in his arms. Through Harry we may sense the overwhelming grief of Wallace for his great friend. Graham's body was carried to the churchyard of Falkirk, where his resting place is marked still by a gravestone and inscription, several times renewed. Sir John Stewart is said to lie nearby, his grave marked by a plain stone without inscription.[4]

Leaving his soldiers to their gruesome task among the dead, with ten men Wallace set out in the small hours for Dunipace. His mood was black and his heart heavy. Bruce arrived at the appointed hour and received a further rebuke for his part in the slaughter. But he had undergone a change of heart. Learning this, knight bent the knee to nobleman. They retired to converse privately and Harry cannot tell exactly what took place. But some men present were in the know, he says, and assert the intention of Bruce to leave Edward when his bond to the King expired. Writers who accept the presence of Bruce at Falkirk find 'nothing improbable' in the conversations. The gallantry of the sentiments expressed by Wallace 'struck the generous mind of Bruce' and opened his eyes to the honourable course he must take, say the romantics. Hume adds a note: 'This story is told by all Scotch writers, though it must be owned that Trivet and Hemingburgh, authors of good credit, both agree that Bruce was not at that time in Edward's army.'[5]

It has been argued that the battle need never have been fought, and here again may be seen the influence of Lord Hailes. 'If the Scots' he says, 'had studied to protract the campaign instead of hazarding a general action at Falkirk . . .' His remark on 'the fatal precipitancy of the Scots' is all but a contradiction of another, that their army this day 'stood on the defensive'. But for the intervention of the two Scottish earls who betrayed them, might they not, as

Hailes concludes, 'have foiled the whole power of Edward and forced him to the necessity of an inglorious retreat'?[6]

In his examination of the battle, Fergusson points out that the dispositions were exactly the same as those that won Waterloo[7] in June 1815, 'even to the rearward position of Wallace's horse!'[8] Historians are agreed, however, that the longbow won Falkirk. Drawn to the ear of the archer instead of the chest, it had greater momentum than earlier weapons. First used by the Welsh, learned and adapted by the English, it made obsolete time-honoured methods of warfare.

Edward remained in Scotland a further two weeks. He had won a battle but little else, and 'only one knight lost' is scarcely credible. Lack of supplies prevented any notable follow-up by the English, though Edward installed a strong garrison and repaired Stirling Castle. Going west to Ayr and finding the castle there destroyed by Bruce, he retaliated by storming through Annandale and burning Lochmaben Castle. Across the Border at Carlisle he held a council where the distribution of Scottish lands to deserving knights and officers – or the promise, since much of the country was firmly in Scots hands – caused displeasure among his barons. Yet again it was the great Earls of Norfolk, Hereford, and Lincoln who rebelled against the King and marched off to their domains in the south.

The Scots at once began the recovery of lands and possessions. A letter from Sir John de Kingston, Constable of Edinburgh Castle, to the Lord Treasurer, dated 9 August, reports, 'the great lords and Earls who were the other side of the Scots water [the Forth] have come to this side . . . and intend to go towards the borders . . .' Edward was losing almost all that he had gained, though provisions and military supplies were being stockpiled in the castles he still held. He would return next year to complete the conquest of Scotland. It must have been with a mixture of exasperation and relief that he turned his back on that troublesome country and led his army home to the rejoicing in London for his victory over Wallace.

# Chapter IX

Shortly after his defeat at Falkirk, Wallace resigned the Guardianship. Detractors would simply relieve him of his post, while eulogists accept the account given by Fordun that 'he chose to serve the crowd, than to be set over them, to their ruin, and the grievous wasting of the people'. How soon after Falkirk is not clear, when 'of his own accord, by the Waters of Forth, he laid down the office which he held' and returned to guerilla warfare. Before the Christmas of 1298, at any rate, Robert Bruce, Earl of Carrick, and Sir John Comyn, Lord of Badenoch, became joint Guardians in his place. The election of these two might be taken as exoneration of their previous behaviour; more likely – as neither was prepared to serve under the governorship of the other – was it a shrewd move by the assembly to drop both into the melting pot in the hope of achieving a more harmonious brew?

It was near to Christmas of one year, so Harry says, that news came to Wallace of the death of his mother. Driven once more from her home at Ellerslie, she sought refuge at the shrine of St Margaret at Dunfermline, where she died. Unable to attend her at the last, he sent Jop and John Blair to see that due homage was paid to her.

> 'Better he thought that it should happen so;
> No Southron should her put to other woe.'
> *[Book X, lines 843–844]*

The persecution of his mother during his Guardianship is unthinkable without some notable retribution. This sad event may be placed near the end of 1298 or, more probably, in some later year after his return from France.

Harry sends his hero twice to that country. The first visit was, he claims, at the invitation of Philip IV, and on 20 April, when 'fresh Flora her flowery mantle spread', Wallace, with a few close friends and a company of fifty, set sail from Kirkcudbright in a bright new barge. Knowing that his departure would be opposed in some quarters at home, and also to avoid possible interception by the English, he did not make public his intentions. After a day and a half at sea, the master from his lookout sighted sixteen vessels under the blood-red flag of the notorious pirate, the Red Rover. Capture was certain, as no ship could escape his fast one and no crew withstand the strength of his boarding party. The worried master explained the pirate's methods and Wallace vowed 'to rid the narrow seas of this rover'. Placing the barge under charge of his own men, Kneland to steer and Craufurd to the mainsail, with a dozen more he lay on the deck out of sight. In full armour the Rover boarded the vessel with his jubilant crew, to be surprised by a band of men accustomed to fighting and winning against heavy odds. Wallace dealt with the pirate chief by compressing the steel collar round his throat, till he could make only signs for mercy. His men threw down their arms and their lives were spared. The pirate then told his story: his name was Thomas de Longueville, a Frenchman banished from court for slaying another. For sixteen years he had been at sea, plundering ships and terrorising the ports. His courage and strength was such that he believed himself the master of any man – except Wallace, the redeemer of Scotland. Wallace heard him out and offered terms of peace, then he said:

> '"I am that man that you advance so hie;
> And bot schort tyme sen I com to the se;
> Of Scotland born; my right name is Wallace."'
> *[Book IX, lines 373–375]*

At this Longueville fell on his knees, promising lifelong service to his captor and to Scotland, and his ships to escort the barge into the harbour at Rochelle. Warned by church bells and trumpets that the pirate fleet was approaching, the citizens prepared to fight or to flee. Wallace ordered that his vessel alone should first enter port, and, at the sight of the Red Lion of Scotland run up above the pirate flag, the scene changed to one of welcome. The Scots company remained for four days, making preparations for the journey to Paris, where they were warmly received by King Philip and his court. So impressed was the King by his illustrious visitor, and by his capture of the pirate, that he pardoned Longueville and knighted him there and then. True to his word, Sir Thomas returned to Scotland to fight at the side of his champion, and he later became a supporter of Bruce.

Another fictitious adventure? Well, Sir Walter Scott uses 'the history' to illustrate the settlement of the Charteris family in the Castle of Kinfauns. 'We relate it' he says, 'as it is given by an ancient and uniform tradition, which carries in it great indications of truth and is warrant enough, perhaps, for its use in graver histories than the present.'[1] For the beauty as well as the strength of his person, Sir Thomas de Longueville was chosen by the heiress of the ancient family of Charteris to be her husband. She bestowed upon him the baronial castle, and their descendants took the name of Charteris 'though the name of Longueville was equally honoured among them'.

Of further interest in this connection is a colophon at the end of the 1570 edition of Harry's *Wallace*:

Imprentit at Edinburgh be Robert Lekpreuik at the
expensis of Henri Charteris and ar to be sould in
his buith on the north syde of the gate above the Trone.
Anno D° MDLXX[2]

Harry keeps Wallace in France until August, and here again he is not consistent with his own writings or with events. If in fact Wallace paid a courtesy visit to Philip while Guardian of Scotland, it could only have taken place in the spring and early summer of 1298. The charter to Scrymgeour was signed 29 March; if he sailed on 20 April, Wallace had seven weeks to journey to France and return, as he must, to defeat the English at Blackearnside on 12 June. Harry names Longueville present at this fight and at Falkirk.

The second excursion he places immediately after Falkirk. Wallace called a parliament and resigned his office, determined to go to France 'to win his living there', and sailed from Dundee in a merchant ship. Among eighteen close companions are named Edward Little (his sister's son), Symon and Richard Wallace (brothers of Adam of Riccarton), Thomas Gray, Jop, John Blair, Longueville, and the son of the Baron of Brechin. Near the mouth of the Humber a large red sail with 'leopardis standand hie' signalled the approach of the

English pirate, John of Lynn. Blair, the chaplain, appears as a hero in this saga, bringing down one pirate with every arrow shot. He modestly leaves the insertion of his own deeds in his *Latin Buik* to his fellow-priest and witness, Gray. The pirate crew of 140 were disposed of and it is Wallace, naturally, who ends the career of John of Lynn. At Sluys the victors took what gold they needed; the pirate ship and the rest of the cargo were given to the merchants.

Wallace made his way through Flanders to Paris, again warmly received by the King. Nine hundred exiled Scots rallied to the standard of their countryman, and Longueville rounded up many Frenchmen. For the capture of Schenoun and Bordeaux, Philip offered Wallace the Lordship of Guienne, which he declined, but for two years more he remained in France, fighting the English.

We come now to more solid historic ground. In the summer of 1299 William Lamberton, Bishop of St Andrews, went on a mission to France. King Edward directed masters of several ships to watch for and intercept the Bishop on his return passage – unsuccessfully as it turned out, for Lamberton was present at an assembly at Peebles on 19 August 1299. A letter from King Philip to the Guardians praised them for 'their constancy to their king and their shining valour in defence of their native land against injustice. . . . ' Regarding the aid which they ask, he is not unmindful of the old league between their king themselves and him, and is carefully pondering ways and means of helping them.[3]

All the Scots leaders were present except Wallace. Sir David Graham, younger brother of Sir John, demanded the lands and goods of Sir William Wallace because he was going abroad without leave. Sir Malcolm Wallace – still very much alive – objected strongly to the implication that his brother was forsaking the cause. The two accused each other of lying and drew swords. During further arguments Sir John Comyn grabbed Bruce by the throat and Buchan, Comyn's kinsman, 'laid violent hands' on the Bishop, who supported Bruce. Agreement was finally reached that Lamberton should join the Guardians with custody of the castles. A spy at the meeting repeated these matters to Sir Robert Hastings, Captain of Roxburgh, who lost no time in conveying them to Edward. His letter is dated 20 August. Lamberton's recent mission having failed to produce any practical help, Wallace could best serve his country by going himself to seek King Philip's aid. (Can this be Harry's second visit?

not immediately, but a year after Falkirk.)

The Kings of France and England, meanwhile, submitted their disputes to the arbitration of Pope Boniface VIII, and the outcome was a suggestion that Edward marry Philip's half-sister Margaret, and the Prince of Wales marry his daughter Isabella. The French king's insistence that his Scots allies and their king be restored to liberty Edward turned down, but he agreed to abandon his ally the Earl of Flanders if Philip would do the same in respect of King John. Baliol was transferred to the custody of the Pope and allowed to retire to his estate in Normandy.

Murison refers to Bishop Stapleton's *Kalendar of Treasury Documents*, compiled about 1323, in which there is mention of 'certain letters' of safe conduct granted by Philip, King of France; John, King of Scotland; and Haco, King of Norway, to William Wallace, enabling him to go to the realms of the said kings, to sojourn there and to return. And the documents also refer to letters concerning 'ordinances and confederations' written to the said William by certain magnates of Scotland. The letters, found on Wallace when he was captured, were delivered to Edward at Kingston by Sir John Segrave. No dates are preserved and the originals lost.[4]

Edward's own annalist, William Rishanger, states that Philip threw Wallace into prison, requesting Edward to take custody of the former Governor of Scotland. The King of England at the time, preparing for his forthcoming marriage to Margaret of France, was content to leave the rebel where he was. Active intervention by Philip on Scotland's behalf was now out of the question. Wallace was not handed over – if indeed he was ever actually imprisoned – but furnished instead with a letter of recommendation to the Pope. Five hundred years later a document came to the attention of Joseph Stevenson in the Tower of London.[5] The translation here is that given by Murison:

*'Philip, by the grace of God King of the French, to my beloved and trusty agents appointed to the court of Rome, greetings and love. We command you to request the Supreme Pontiff to hold our beloved William Wallace of Scotland, Knight, recommended to his favour in these matters of business that he has to despatch with him.*

*'Given at Pierrepoint on Monday after the Feast of All Saints.'*[6]

The letter is said to be written in a French hand and genuine; it is taken as almost certain proof that Wallace went to France at least once. We need not conclude because he retained the letters that he never made use of them; the *Kalendar* shows the grants of safe conduct were to cover his 'return'. Is it then so wild a conjecture that, somewhere in the dark recesses of the Tower, an anonymous clerk, recording documents taken from the prisoner in 1305, either by accident or design mislaid one of the original letters he was under orders to destroy?

There is no clear evidence that Wallace went to Norway or Rome, only pointers to make the supposition not unreasonable; he had ample time. Bruce was then joint Guardian, his eldest sister, Isobel, Queen of Norway and sympathetic, no doubt, to the Scottish cause. A bull issued by the Pope in June 1299, claiming Scotland as belonging to the Holy See, took over a year to reach Edward. He replied that His Holiness had been deceived by 'certain enemies of peace and sons of rebellion' then resident at his court.[7]

From the meeting at Peebles in August 1299, when we hear of his intended departure, Wallace disappears for a time from the front lines of history. Where was he? 'We are now able to answer that question,' says Stevenson. 'Wallace, during that period did NOT neglect his trust; he did NOT forsake the cause . . . he DID exert himself to the utmost in defence of the fallen and betrayed liberties of his country. . . . Finding no chance of success at home . . . he hastened to plead the cause of Scotland at the throne of France.'[8]

# Chapter X

Following his marriage in 1299, King Edward ratified a truce that was to last until St Andrew's Day, 30 November 1302. Nevertheless, each side continued to harass the other, and castles changed hands, Stirling again to the Scots. A further treaty negotiated with King Philip that included Scotland, ratified by Edward on 30 October 1300, was to last from New Year's Day to Whit Sunday. In that year Bruce resigned the Guardianship 'in disgust'. Sir Ingram de Umfraville, Earl of Angus – one of the partnership that betrayed the Scots' positions before Falkirk – was elected in his place.

Edward returned to the North; any peace overtures made to him only sharpened his temper. Comyn and Buchan tried for two whole days – their terms, that King John be returned and the barons' land be restored to them, made him extremely angry and were refused. The war began again, Scottish nobles employing the formerly despised guerilla tactics of Wallace. Edward was short of money and his efforts to extract more taxes further alienated his barons at home. His army had had enough of the Scottish campaign, Welsh soldiers deserted and the nobles, anxious to return to England, simply packed up and left when their requests for leave were refused. The cruel winter of 1300/1301 Edward spent at Carlisle, to be on hand for the final assault he was determined to launch on Scotland in the spring.

In response to the Pope's bull of 1299, delivered to him in August 1300 by the Archbishop of Canterbury, the King set up his usual elaborate processes of legal investigation, but a parliament at Lincoln on 12 February 1301 rejected absolutely the papal claim, as did the French and Scots, and the bull was burnt. Robert Wishart, Bishop of Glasgow, no doubt influenced by the Pope, in October 1300 renewed allegiance to Edward, and in April 1302 Robert Bruce did the same.

About this time a Scottish knight, Simon Fraser of Tweedale, up to now on the English side, joined his countrymen. He was one of the many knights captured at Dunbar in 1296, 'freedom' the prize dangled before them for service with Edward in France. His loyalty and courage then earned the King's esteem, the restoration of his lands, and the Wardenship of Selkirk Forest. But as early as 1298, in his letter of 9 August to the Lord Treasurer, Sir John de Kingston warned '. . . Fraser is not of such good faith as he ought to be'.[1]

With the ending of the truce in November, both sides prepared for action. Edward was in England and sent into Scotland an army under Sir John Segrave, which, for the purpose of obtaining food and forage, split into three camps. Believing Scottish resistance broken, the English during the winter became less vigilant, and on the first Sunday in Lent were taken completely by surprise. Sir John Comyn, now the sole director of the Scots military affairs and joined by Sir Simon Fraser, near Roslin at daybreak on 24 February 1303 attacked and defeated first the main enemy division and then the other two – three battles and three sections of the English army beaten in one day. In the fury Sir John Segrave was himself badly wounded and captured.

Rishanger attributes the rising of the Scots to Wallace, again their appointed leader. But there is nothing else to support this, and Murison says it would be rash to believe he was present, or that he acted in concert with Comyn.[2] If Wallace was involved in the victory at Roslin, Harry would surely have made much of it.

A Scottish delegation went again to Paris, where they were when the Princess Isabella and the Prince of Wales were betrothed on 20 May 1303, a peace treaty between France and England coinciding with the event. The Scots were excluded, but Philip assured them of his good offices if the envoys failed to procure a truce with Edward.

That king meanwhile had launched his massive campaign and was progressing through Scotland with little opposition. Only two castles resisted him: at Brechin Sir Thomas de Maule mocked the English from the battlements, wiping the walls with a napkin where they were struck by stones from the siege-engines. With his death resistance ended. For the winter of 1303/1304 Edward installed himself in Dunfermline Abbey, 'spacious enough to lodge at one and the same time conveniently three mighty kings and their retinues'. Here lay the remains of his sister Margaret, her husband Alexander

III and their children. Here he could shape laws for Scotland on the English pattern, and merge the smaller nation into the larger; here his dream would become reality, the whole island one ENGLAND. He called a parliament; only three prominent Scots were absent – Sir William Wallace, Sir Simon Fraser, and Sir William Oliphant, Constable of Stirling Castle.

After weeks of negotiation, Sir John Comyn, induced by the deplorable state of the country, the shortage of food, and the benevolent mood of the King at the time, finally accepted terms of submission. At Strathford in Fifeshire on 9 February 1304 the treaty was concluded. Terms of banishment for varying periods were imposed, depending on individual measures of obstinacy. James the Steward, Sir John de Soulis, a former Guardian, and Bishop Wishart, were exiled for two to three years. Simon Fraser, Thomas de Bois, David de Graham and Alexander de Lindsay could purge their sins in three years' exile from Scotland, England, and France. 'As for William Wallace, it is agreed that he shall surrender himself up at the will and mercy of our sovereign Lord the King, if it shall seem good to him.' A letter to the King from Sir Alexander de Abernethy on the subject of Wallace received an answer dated 3 March:

*'In reply to your request for instructions as to whether it is our pleasure that you should hold out to William Wallace any words of peace: know that it is not in our pleasure that you hold out any words of peace to him or to any other of his company, unless they place themselves absolutely and in all things at our will without any reservation whatsoever.'*

Murison says there is nothing to show whether Sir Alexander put the point to Edward on his own motion, or was prompted to do so from the Scottish side; he adds, 'it is not to be believed for an instant that any such application would have been made with the sanction or knowledge of Wallace himself'.[3] According to the chronicler Bower (Fordun), he was offered lordships and lands, and his friends, urging their acceptance, were answered always in the same vein, with the proverb learned as a youth from his uncle, and the following sentiments:

"If you were to judge as I do, you would not readily place your neck under a foreign yoke. . . . I declare that if all Scotland together yield obedience to the King of England, or part each one with his own liberty, yet I and my comrades who may be willing to adhere to me in this behalf, will stand for the freedom of the realm; and with God's help we will obey no man but the King or his lieutenant."

Langtoft's chronicle, 'improved' by Robert de Brunne, alleges that after the Christmas of 1303 Wallace lay in hiding in the forest and 'through friends' sought terms of peace, beseeching Edward to yield him an allowance of woods, cattle and horses, that he might honourably keep and hold in heritage, in return for peaceful submission. This demand is said to have made Edward 'fulle grim' and in a rage he promised 300 marks to any man who shall 'bring his hede to toun'. Then, says the chronicler, the outlaw flew to the moors and hills and sustained himself through robbery. This is the only statement, Fergusson says, that Wallace ever made any attempt to come to terms.[4] And however bold his character, such a proposal, argues Paterson, 'is not consistent with the testimony of those who knew him best'.

These matters bring to the fore the whole question of Wallace's whereabouts during this period. An absence of seven years – from Falkirk to the year of his capture – can be discounted. Edward would not have made specific terms in respect of an absent and forgotten rebel. If Rishanger is right, and Wallace was behind events culminating in the battles at Roslin, then Harry's term of two years abroad seems nearer the truth and would bring Wallace home in 1301–1302 to campaign in the north rather than the south, where Comyn held sway.

The sailing from Arbroath of Squire Guthrie settles more convincingly into this period. Landing in Flanders he finds Wallace eventually in Guienne, and relating to him the plight of his country urges his return. Philip reluctantly lets him go, showering him with gifts and letters already received from magnates in Scotland requesting the presence of Wallace at home. Guthrie's barge sails from Sluys and lands Wallace and his party of eighteen at Montrose.

To this episode, perhaps, may be linked his concealment in the barn of his cousin, William Craufurd. Arousing suspicion in St Johnston, where he was observed purchasing more provisions than usual, Craufurd was thrown into prison. The extras, he explained, were for a 'kyrkyn feast', a thanksgiving after a wife's confinement. But news of Wallace's return was flashing through the country; Craufurd was allowed to go home, but hastily armed men under Sir

John Butler soon followed his tracks. In nearby Elcho Park, Wallace again made use of the trees, weaving branches into an impenetrable 'strength' and dividing his men into three groups to defend it, six to Longueville, six to Craufurd, and to himself the other five. The Scots had no food, and water only from a stream. This Butler knew, and having failed to capture his enemy in fight, tried persuasion. Wallace answered:

> '"I sall cum out at that ilk place to morn,
> Or ellys to nycht; traist weill quhat I the say;
> I byd noght here till nyne houris off the day."'
> *[Book XII, lines 494–496]*

The English would wait; 800 surrounded the wood and settled down for the night. Towards dawn a thick mist enveloped the countryside the Scots knew so well, and their ever watchful leader formed his plan. Sir John's positions being then only lightly guarded, they fought their way out and the third-generation Butler fell to the sword of Wallace. Craufurd was badly wounded in the knee and unable to walk; Wallace carried him under his arm – for nine acres, Harry says – before setting him down. In Methven Wood they could appease their hunger, and joined by other outlawed knights they passed into Lorn, an area already stripped of meat and vegetation. Wallace reproached himself for the near starvation of his men, and, greatly distressed, set off alone to hunt. He sat down under an oak, leaning his sword and bow against it, and soon fell asleep. Five men, three English, two Scots, set to keep watch on him, seized the opportunity to bind and take him alive, and claim the promised rewards. But the 'manliest man living' was not to be held down by five lesser men; Wallace sprang to his feet and quickly disposed of three while the others fled, and, since Harry claims that 'none living might pass from him on foot', the two were soon caught and slain. A boy carrying their provisions returned with Wallace to his camp, where, with 'great cheer', roast meat, bread, and cheese were dealt out to the hungry men.

From Lorn they moved on to Rannoch, all there being prepared to serve under Wallace's command. In two days an army 7,000-strong, horsed and equipped, and with banners raised, moved to Dunkeld, into Ross and on to Aberdeen. From their places of exile or hiding came Boyd, Lindsay, Seton, Lauder, Sinclair, Richard de

Lundin, and Adam Wallace. It was the Bishop of Dunkeld, Harry says, who hastened to Edward in London with news of this fresh uprising.

By March 1304 the King's business at Dunfermline was completed. The Scots had in times past used the abbey for their assemblies, and this was excuse enough for the building to be destroyed. As Edward departed, the magnificent abbey went up in flames. Now for Stirling Castle: by his command there was to be no exchange of business or merchandise, no communication whatsoever between people outside and the garrison within. Siege-engines, stones and iron, ordered from Glasgow, Edinburgh and other towns were to be delivered to Stirling 'without excuse or delay', and the Prince of Wales was made responsible for the stripping of lead from church roofs.

Wallace and Fraser joined forces again, hopefully to get relief or assistance to the castle, but the Forth was too heavily guarded and they could not cross. Segrave, Bruce, and Clifford, guided to their camp by one John de Mussellburgh, defeated the two at Peebles, but they escaped. Three days later the treacherous Mussellburgh, a Scot, received ten shillings from the King's own hand. Attempts by Wallace and Fraser to draw off pressure from the castle had little effect, and on 22 April 1304 the assault began, Edward directing operations with youthful zest, often exposing himself to danger.

For three months the garrison held out while the castle was pounded by thirteen siege-engines, hurling weights of up to 300 pounds. Only when it was reduced to a pile of rubble, and its defenders to 'the utmost extremity' by famine, did the gallant commander surrender, on 24 July. Before his soldiers entered the ruins, Edward put on a show for Queen Margaret and her ladies, watching from a specially prepared lookout. His new engine, the War-Wolf, had yet to be tried and the unfortunate garrison were made to endure further bombardment before being paraded – barefoot and wearing only their shirts – to bend the knee to the conqueror. Their lives were spared, to be spent in English dungeons.

The siege was said by the English to be the most obstinate of the war. Sir William Oliphant, captured at Dunbar, was imprisoned in Devizes Castle until 8 September 1297. Returning to Scotland, his patriotic endeavours earned him the command of the country's most important fortress. Valour was rewarded now in the Tower of London by his being 'not chained'.[5] Released in an exchange of prisoners, this courageous man returned to fight yet again. He died in 1329.

1304 saw the submission to Edward of the Scots leaders: Comyn, young Bruce, Lamberton, and finally Fraser. An English scribe asserts, 'there was left but one disorderly fellow, William Wallace by name, who gave the king just a touch of uneasiness'.[5] That 'touch' Edward knew well would stand in the way of the complete subjugation of Scotland. It must be removed. So earnestly did he desire the capture of Wallace that, after the fall of Stirling Castle, he decreed shortened terms of exile and reduced ransoms to Comyn, Lindsay, Graham, Fraser, and others, who could trap him 'between now and the twentieth day after Christmas'. To their eternal credit, Murison says, 'they do not appear – not one of them – to have taken a single step to better or shield themselves by ignominious treachery to their undaunted friend'. One of the Scots captured at Stirling Castle, Ralph de Haliburton, was released from prison on 28 February 1305 and taken to Scotland 'to help in the capture of Sir William Wallace'. It stands on record that Sir John de Mobray and others gave security to re-enter Ralph at the parliament in London three weeks after Easter (18 April) 'after seeing what he can do'.[6] However familiar he was with the haunts and habits of Wallace, he does not appear to have done very much. Perhaps his contribution was yet to come.

Robert Bruce, 6th Lord of Annandale, died in 1304. His eldest son, Robert, Earl of Carrick, now thirty years of age, although in Edward's peace and sometimes at his court, prepared to claim the throne of Scotland. He signed a secret pact of mutual assistance with Bishop Lamberton – five weeks after the Bishop's submission to Edward. Crown and Church together – if his plan was to succeed Bruce needed to win support from the people. For that he must have Wallace, and he informed him of his intentions. The growing comradeship between them does not rest on the testimony of the Minstrel alone. The charter of 1298, granting lands and offices to Alexander Scrymgeour, was confirmed by Bruce in 1303. Fergusson points out that he names Wallace in baronial style – the highest compliment he could pay him – at a time when Wallace had fallen from power and Bruce was himself under allegiance to Edward.[7] Both documents are extant. After the resignation of Wallace, Lamberton ordered a portion of his own stipend from St Andrews to be set aside for the sustenance of the former Guardian, to whom he remained a loyal friend.

In some writings one senses criticism of Wallace for backing a loser – a lack of sound judgement on his part. Baliol was not a loser, but the lawfully appointed crowned King of Scotland. Once it became clear that he would not return, the indications are that Wallace was ready to serve a future king with the same wholeheartedness. Harry, at any rate, shows him anxious for Bruce to claim the crown, sending Jop into England with a letter urging him to do so. Bruce replies 'with hys owin hand' thanking Wallace for his loyalty and kindness and beseeching his counsel:

'For he behoved out of Ingland to steill;
For lang befor was kepyt the ragment
Which Comyn had, to byd the gret parlement
Into London; and if thai hym accus
To cum frai thaim, he suld mak sum excus.
He prayit Wallace in Glasgow moor to walk
The first nyght of July for hys sak.'
*[Book XII, lines 974–980]*

Because of their mutual dislike and distrust, there was between Bruce and Comyn – in the present day idiom – no friendly dialogue. Riding together one day from Stirling, however, they learned of their manipulation by King Edward, who, Buchanan remarks, 'had thus obtained their assistance in the reduction of Scotland'. An agreement was drawn up, mutually signed and sworn. Bruce should obtain the crown, Comyn yielding up his right to him; and Comyn should receive the large and opulent estates which belonged to Bruce in Scotland, and be held next in rank to the King.[8] They pledged themselves to each other and to secrecy, and to await an opportunity to effect their plan. This bond, if it be the 'ragment' mentioned, Fordun attributes to 1304. The request from Bruce that Wallace meet him in July can only mean 1305, and Harry's lines reflect the suspicion felt then of Comyn's good faith. The letter from Bruce was greatly pleasing to Wallace and he promptly moved his household to Glasgow for a month. By this Harry means, no doubt, his personal attendants, arms and horses, and the wherewithal for their existence in the forests.

Meanwhile, disturbed by the news from Scotland, Edward sent for Sir Aymer de Valence, to discuss what best to do about Wallace. If someone could be found to deceive him, he could be captured and put down. Valence returned to Scotland with Edward's support for any course of action he found necessary. Harry's story is of a bribe, £3,000 in gold, to any man who could be persuaded to undertake the task. Sir John Menteith, Constable of Dumbarton Castle and sheriff of that shire, appeared to be interested and consented to a meeting with Valence in Ruglen Kirk. The Minstrel allows Menteith some reluctance:

"' . . . He is our governor;
For us he stood in many a felon stour;
Not for himself but for our heritage:
To sell him thus it war a foul outrage."'
*[Book XII, lines 809–812]*

Outrage he may have expressed and even felt, but he agreed to the plan on the promise that the life of Wallace be spared, and no suspicion was aroused when he put his sister's son to the service of the Chief, with instructions to watch and report his movements. In de Brunne's chronicle the youth is named as Jak Schort, chosen for the task because, his brother having been slain by Wallace, he was prepared to do him mischief.

So, with Kerlie and the young spy, Wallace rode out on Glasgow Moor on the first night of July, expecting to meet Bruce, who must have found difficulty in getting out of England. The eighth time Menteith knew the pattern. With sixty men 'of his own kin' he waited for the three to return. Wallace and Kerlie went to sleep while the youth kept watch. He removed their weapons and gave the arranged signal. Kerlie was immediately slain. Wallace, after feeling for the sword that never left his side, defended himself with his hands. Knowing he would rather die than be taken prisoner, Menteith came forward and told him resistance was in vain; the house was surrounded by men who had no wish to harm him. He would be safe in the quarters that still were his in Dumbarton Castle. The English, said Menteith,

'"ask no more but to be quit of your strife"'.
*[Book XII, line 1042]*

Still doubting, Wallace made him swear on oath. That done, he gave up his hands to his captors. His sword Menteith carried off to

Dumbarton Castle as a prized trophy.

No time was lost in bearing the prisoner away from his native land and from any chance of rescue by his supporters. Not daring to pass through areas held by Scots, the party proceeded with all speed, not to Dumbarton but southward, and, with Kerlie missing, Wallace soon realised he had been betrayed.

The place of capture is said to be the house of one Ralph Raa, in or near Glasgow, on Thursday 5 August 1305.

At Solway Sands he was handed over to Valence and Clifford, carried to Carlisle, presumably on horseback, and thrown into prison there under the custody of Sir John Segrave. The journey to London used normally to take about fourteen days; the messenger bearing the news made greater haste, for when the cavalcade arrived the capital was in carnival mood to receive the notorious outlaw.

On Sunday 22 August, Sir John Segrave rode into London, his prisoner heavily chained in accordance with King Edward's strict command. So great was the crowd anxious to gaze on the rebel that he could not be taken to the Tower, but was lodged for the night in the house of William de Lyre, a citizen of Fenchurch Street. Next morning, accompanied by sheriffs and aldermen of the City of London – as Fergusson puts it, 'with the retinue of a king'[9] – Wallace was taken to Westminster Hall and seated on the south bench. A crown of laurel was placed on his head. Other prisoners, Llewelyn of Wales before him and Simon Fraser after, were adorned in the same manner, suggesting common practice rather than a special insult to Wallace 'to deride him for a remark he is said to have made, that he deserved to wear a crown in that Hall'. And the remark, recorded by Matthew of Westminster, if made at all, is perfectly in tune with the occasional flashes of humour attributed to Wallace in Harry's poem.

All was prepared: the King's Chief Justice, Sir Peter Malorie, read out the terrible indictment. Having always known what his fate would be if captured, Wallace listened in silence, replying only to the charge of 'traitor to the King of England', which he denied, 'in so much as being no subject, never having sworn homage, he could not be guilty of treason'. The recital goes on: "that John Baliol (never referred to as King though Edward decreed him so) having forfeited the kingdom of Scotland, Edward conquered it and publicly received the homage of its prelates, barons, earls, and others – that the aforesaid William Wallace, forgetting his allegiance and fealty, had raised an immense body of followers, had attacked the English officers, had slain William de Heselrigg whose dead body he afterwards cut into pieces – that gaining strength and influence he stormed the English garrisons, caused his writs to run through Scotland as if he were superior lord of that realm, that he summoned parliament, that he attempted to league himself with the King of France, ravaged Northumberland, Cumberland, and Westmorland, slaughtered the people, opposed the king in a pitched battle and when defeated refused to avail himself of the terms of peace held out to his acceptance". He was therefore outlawed.

"And since it is inconsistent with the laws of England that one so outlawed . . . should be admitted to defend himself or plead . . ." sentence of death was accordingly pronounced upon him: "to be hanged, drawn, and quartered, disembowelled and all internal organs whence such perverted thoughts proceed to be cast into the fire and burnt. The head to be set up on London Bridge; one quarter to be hung on a gibbet over the public sewers at Newcastle-upon-Tyne, the others at Berwick, Stirling, and St Johnston, as a warning to all who behold them."

Wallace is said to have asked for a priest in order to make confession. In the Minstrel's account, the King threatened the clergy with loss of life should any be so bold "yon tyrant for to shrive". The Archbishop of Canterbury defied him utterly. He would himself hear confession and administer the sacrament, and if force was employed to prevent him, he would make it known that the King was a heretic. Edward demanded the Archbishop's arrest, but his lords counselled otherwise. All Englishmen present, they said, thought the priest was in the right. In sight of them all he heard the prisoner's confession and commended his spirit to God, before riding away to the 'West Monastery', wanting no further part in the proceedings. Wallace was then lashed to a hurdle and dragged along at ground level by horses, through the rough streets, first to the Tower and on to the Elms at Smithfield, a journey of four miles. It was at the gallows, Harry says, that he was 'stripped of his weid' and, told to name his last wish, requested of the 'Lord Clifford' that the psalter he had carried with him since childhood be held open before him by a priest, 'until they had done to him all that they would'. This was granted against Edward's express order that no comfort be afforded him. Antagonism between the King and Archbishop Winchelsea is well known, and Sir Robert Clifford was one of Wallace's custodians: there seems little reason to doubt the accuracy of Harry's report.

The sentence was carried out to the letter, barbaric indignities inflicted prior to the hanging, the butchers being masters at their craft of keeping a prisoner alive to endure the maximum suffering. His still-living body was cut down and disembowelled, the entrails burnt. When he had passed beyond all feeling, his torturers cut off his head and hacked his body into four quarters. 'The death of Wallace' writes Burton, 'stands forth among the violent ends which have a memorable place in history. Proverbially such acts belong to a policy that outwits itself. But the retribution has seldom come so quickly, and so utterly in defiance of all human preparation and calculation, as here.'[10]

The account still exists of fifteen shillings – cut to ten – paid to Sir John Segrave for 'transporting the remains of William le Waleys to Scotland' and the completion of his gruesome errand. Forty marks were given to the person who watched Wallace; 60 marks to those present at the capture, 'that the King desires shall be divided among them'. Land to the value of £100 was assigned to Sir John Menteith. 'We shall not overstate the amount thus distributed' says Stevenson, 'if we consider it equivalent to £1100 of ready money. This is exclusive of Sir John Menteith's share of the spoil, the amount of which is not easy to reckon since it was expended in land.

'We have here the documentary testimony of an eyewitness probably – certainly of a contemporary writer, and of one whose official position in the City of London made him well acquainted with the whole of the details, which he preserved. Accordingly, we find that whatever information can be added to it from documents of undisputed authenticity fully supports its general correctness and substantiates its details.'[11]

To an anonymous English scribe again we are indebted for the report that when Wallace was brought before the King, Edward would not look at him; he would not demean himself, is one explanation. Why then did he insist on bringing the outlaw to London? Why not hang him at Newcastle and have done with him? The question invites speculation. This challenge to the divine right of kings must be stamped out in the most brutal and humiliating manner. With the gallows already erected especially high 'so that the people might see', the sentence prepared, the punishment prescribed, the 'trial' was just another display of legality.

The Prince of Wales was twenty-one, his passion for Piers Gaveston caused not only grave disturbance in the land, but sickened and angered his father. The King's only brother, Edmund, was known as 'Crouchback', *his* son as 'Henry Wry-Neck', nicknames that suggest deformities, though not serious enough to hamper Edmund, an active warrior. These were the men closest to Edward. Now sixty-six, worn from the burdens of kingship and a life of almost continuous fighting, embittered and lonely, he comes at last face to face with the man who had thwarted his ambition. The privations Wallace endured after his capture must have taken their toll of even his prodigious stamina, but this giant of a man in his early thirties still held in his own land what Edward had forfeited at home: the love of the common people. Was it from hatred alone that he averted his gaze? Did he see in his prisoner the man he once was, the man he so dearly wanted a son of his to be? From the time of Queen Eleanor's death his family life deteriorated. Even in the matter of a second wife he had to settle for second best. The twenty-four-year-old Blanche, most beautiful of King Philip's sisters, spurned the elderly King of England for a younger man, and on 8 September 1299, although three times her age, Edward married Margaret[12] – and was luckier than he knew! Mindful always of the succession, and with only one surviving son, he would have his wife accompany him. The gentle young queen saw for herself the desolation of Scotland, her sympathy the natural outcome of long friendship between that country and her own. Indeed, the earlier two-year truce is said to have been brought about through her mediation, her presence at Stirling to witness the fall of the castle and the humiliation of its defenders but another example of the King's petulance. Is it here that 'something peculiar' Dr Lingard finds in the case of Wallace, 'making him less deserving of Edward's mercy'? If there can be found one spark of human feeling behind the spite and vindictiveness that consumed this once great man and splendid king, we may spare for him some of the compassion he denied his greatest adversary, for in the Knight of Ellerslie, Edward Plantagenet had met his match.

Other privileges granted to Menteith were a place at the English parliament vacated by the Earl of March, and at the request of his 'loyal and faithful John' Edward issued letters of safe conduct to last two to three years, as well as a charter granting to him the Earldom of Lennox. Buchanan tells of Menteith's further treachery

– to Bruce, whom he later served well and from whom he procured pardon for his former deeds.[13] Legend has it that after the death of Wallace, at any banquet attended by a Menteith the knives and forks were placed with points facing the sitter. The practice is said to have continued for three to four hundred years – through the Stewart Dynasty in fact, and almost to the Union of Kingdoms in 1707: Menteith was a Stewart, and it is hard to believe that the discourtesy would for so long be displayed to members of the ruling family, or be tolerated by them – unless as a sop to public opinion.

A popular version of the capture, in which Wallace visits a tavern frequented by English soldiers, his presence betrayed to them by Menteith turning the bread on the table, has no place in the leading biographies. It is totally unconvincing in the light of Wallace's proven sagacity.

Robert Bruce, according to the Minstrel, returned to Scotland three days after the capture. Greatly distressed, he went to Lochmaben, where his brother Edward delivered a comforting eulogy:

'"Let mourning be; it may mak na remeid;
Ye haiff hym lost, ye suld revenge his deid.
Bot for your caus he tuk the war on hand
In your defens; and thryce has freed Scotland.
The which was lost fra us and all our kyn:
Were nocht Wallace, we nevir entryt in."'
*[Book XII, lines 1165–1170]*

Also present was the Frenchman, Longueville, whose grief, Harry says, was 'extreme'. He vowed never to return to France but to fight the English in Scotland, and revenge the loss of his hero and friend.

# Chapter XI

What was he really like, this unconquerable Scot? We can but piece together the fragments and form an impression. Here it is of a studious, sensitive youth, deeply affected firstly by the persecution of his family, changed by fortune and circumstance into a stern man and resolute fighter. One of a circle of brothers, cousins, relatives and friends of the knightly class, the middle rank of society, Adam, eldest son of Sir Richard Wallace of Riccarton, Chief of the Name, was the obvious leader of such a group. But to William, the biggest and brainiest, leadership would come naturally in boyhood, and just as naturally be accepted by the others. He was a man of action rather than words, not lacking humour, 'a bit of a devil', never one to resist a challenge.

As to his appearance, historians remind us *there is no contemporary description*.[1] The rather fulsome representation given in a later edition of Fordun's *Scotichronicon* cannot outdo the superb phrase believed to be the original: 'wonderously brave and bold, of goodly mien, and boundless liberality'. Although written after his death and in the light of his martyrdom, it agrees with that given by Harry from his 'auctor' Blair. Envoys from France, seeking Wallace's aid for Philip, are said to have brought with them a description of the Scottish champion by clerks, knights, and heralds of that country, and this, Harry claims, Blair 'set down in Wallas buik'.

'The wit of France thocht Wallace to commend;
In to Scotland, with this harrald thai send
Part of his deed, and als the description
Of hym tayn there, by men of discretion.
Clerkis, knights, and harralds, that hym saw;

Bot I hereof can nocht reherss thaim aw.
Wallace statur, in largeness, and in height,
Was judged thus, by such as saw hym right.
Both in hys armour bright, and in undress,
Nine quarters large he was, in length, no less;
Third part length in shoulders broad was he,
Right seemly, strong, and worthy for to see;
Hys limbs were gret, with stalwart pace and sound:
Hys brows were hard, hys armis were gret and round;
Hys handis right like a palmers did appear,
Of manly mak, with nails both gret and clear.
Proportioned long and fair was his visage;
Right grave of speech, and able in courage;
Broad breast and high, with sturdy neck and gret;
Lips round, hys nose square and proportionate.
Brown wavy hair, on brows and eyebros light,
Eyes clear and piercing, like to diamonds bright.
On the left side was seen below the chin,
By hurt, a wen; his colour was sanguine.
Wounds too, he had, in many a diverse place,
But fair and well preserved was aye hys face.
Of riches for himself he kept no thing;
Gave as he won, like Alexander the King.
In time of peace, meek as a maid was he;
When war approached, the right Hector was he.
To Scotsmen ever credence gret he gave;
Known enemies could never hym deceive.
These qualities of hys were known in France,
Where people held hym in good remembrance.'
*[Book X, lines 1215–1248]*

So what we have is third-hand, but it is *all* we have. The main objection to it is that there can be seen no reason for such a course of action by the French emissaries. A perfectly proportioned figure of six feet nine inches the sceptics find hard to take. 'By what other means indeed' asks Murison, 'could a mere youth . . . uncountenanced by the support of a single great noble . . . have maintained himself, attracted adherents, impressed the enemy, and become the hero of a nation, if he did not possess quite exceptional physical strength and prowess?'[2] The English document in which his name first appears, affirms, as we have seen, that he was a 'mighty' man. There is more reason to accept than to deny his almost gigantic stature.[3] Only the Minstrel's disguises stretch credulity.

Towards the end of his poem Harry expresses a hope that someone with more 'wit and eloquence' may write of Wallace's life. Blair's *Latin Buik* was confirmed, he says, by Bishop Sinclair of Dunkeld, himself a witness to much that Wallace had done, whose purpose was to send the book to the Pope in Rome. But Blair and Gray, who had known Wallace from his sixteenth to his twenty-ninth year, thought the matter might not be pleasing to all. Harry in his time thought it wrong that the deeds of Wallace be smothered and, although himself unlearned, did the best he could, without reward for his labours. He closes his chronicle:

'Now besek God that giver is of grace
Made hell and erth and set the nevyn abuff,
That he us grant of hys der lasting luff.'
*[Book XII, lines 1462–1464]*

Wallace was without doubt in advance of his time, his learning and education possibly superior to that of the sons of nobles who had less need of it. That he would have made his mark in some other sphere also goes undoubted. A magnetic personality and qualities of leadership evoked the jealousy of the barons before any major successes caused them to assume, wrongly, that he was aspiring to the throne. His 'crime' was that he, second son of a second son – and he an obscure knight – should teach the arts of war to the nobles whose responsibility it was. It was not to be tolerated. Far from being headstrong and overbearing, there are numerous incidents of thoughtful planning, of patience and restraint – Stirling Bridge the supreme example. 'His soldiers' remarks Buchanan, 'shrank from no danger under his direction, for his boldness was never rash or unsuccessful.'[4] Burton sees him as 'a man of vast political and military genius,' and 'as a soldier, one of those marvellously gifted men, arising at long intervals, who can see through the military superstitions of the day, and organise power out of those elements which the pedantic soldier rejects as rubbish'.[5] A general at war in defence of his own land and people, to their enemies he was a terrorist. Great cruelty there must have been, but war *is* cruel, and who in this present age of sophisticated destruction shall judge the medieval warrior with but three weapons at his disposal, bow and arrow, sword, and fire?

Did Moray, Douglas or Bruce use them with any less ferocity than did Wallace? Did King Edward? Now, as then, double standards abound. The most casual observer of this blood-soaked era will not fail to notice that barbarism wears other guises when perpetrated by kings and nobles – and usually in the name of God! Edward's treatment of Bruce's womenfolk is almost beyond belief, and one hopes never in all history to find a more cruel fate than befell his son, Edward II, at the possible instigation of his queen, Isabella, the 'she-wolf of France' and her lover Roger Mortimer, and at the hands of their henchmen.

Acts of war apart, Wallace does not appear to have indulged in or permitted cruelty *for its own sake*. Murison is emphatic; he goes so far as to suggest that the behaviour of Wallace, particularly towards the priors at Hexham, may have won over the old chronicler Hemingburgh, since from that episode he drops the term *ille latro* (variously translated as robber, cut-throat, or notorious bandit). Further English testimony allows that Wallace was 'an humane and generous foe'. And the Scottish historian, John Major: 'towards all unwarlike persons, such as women and children, towards all who claimed his mercy, he showed himself humane', the 'the proud and all who offered resistance he knew well how to curb'.[6]

What could he not have gained for himself and those closest to him had he accepted Edward's peace, lordships and lands? and how quickly his 'barbaric' deeds would have been transformed into acts of honour and heroism by the cloistered chroniclers of England! The only suggestion that he ever acquired anything for himself comes in the quarrel at Peebles between his brother Malcolm and Sir David Graham over lands and goods bestowed on their Guardian by a grateful populace.

Throughout his career there is one feature, one word, which more than any other gives the measure of the man: affection. That of his men for their courageous leader, his for them – for the few nobles who adhered to him, and for the ordinary people (men and women), who followed and sustained him, at the pinnacle of power or in extremity. With treachery and intrigue commonplace, father against son, brother against brother, mother against son, and vice versa, the loyalty of Wallace's family is remarkable. The friends he started out with remained, if not at his side, at his call, the faithful Kerlie to the last. After his death even those who out of envy or jealousy withheld their support or hindered his efforts, came to realise his tremendous contribution, the self-sacrifice, iron self-discipline, and, above all, his pure selfless patriotism. All that can be claimed politically is that his sympathies were royalist. For ten months he ruled Scotland; kings have reigned for less, and it is Major who provides the indomitable incorruptible leader with his finest epitaph: 'born as he was of no illustrious house, he yet proved himself a better ruler in the simple armour of his integrity than any of those nobles would have been'.[7]

What irony! that in 1320 the united baronage of Scotland, under Bruce, should send to Pope John XXII a letter, known thereafter as *The Declaration of Arbroath*, beseeching his intervention in the matter of Edward II's aggression against 'little Scotland, which has no refuge but the sea . . . and so long as a hundred of us remain alive, never shall we be subjected to the domination of the English. It is not for glory, riches, or honour, that we fight, but for freedom alone, which no good man lets go, save with his life.'

Bishops Wishart of Glasgow, and Lamberton of St Andrews – as much for the inconsistency of their oath-keeping as for their support for the patriots – served terms of exile in Porchester and Winchester Castles; Boyd, Fraser, Hay, Kirkpatrick, Lindsay, Seton, Scrymgeour, the Earl of Atholl, Earl Malcolm of Lennox, and Adam Wallace, are prominent among the Bruce supporters. Seton, as already stated, paid the supreme penalty at Dumfries in 1306; Scrymgeour, taken prisoner while carrying King Robert's banner at the Battle of Methven, was hanged at Newcastle that same year. Fraser, hanged, drawn and quartered in London, had his head piked on London Bridge; and the Earl of Atholl, because of his rank, was strung up on gallows thirty feet high. The precise fate of Sir Malcolm Wallace, William's elder brother, is not known, other than that he was 'killed by the English';[8] and Sir John, executed in London in 1307, had his head 'raised with shouts near the head of his brother William the Wicked' on London Bridge. So states the chronicle of Langtoft.[9] The Wallaces of Ellerslie were no more, and their estates passed to the family at Riccarton.[10]

# Chapter XII

The winter of 1305/1306 found Robert Bruce again in London at Edward's court, forbidden to leave and with guards set to watch and report his every move. Had some incriminating document been found on Wallace? Did the King know of the secret pact between him – Bruce – and Comyn? Whatever the reason, Bruce felt himself in imminent danger, and when he received from his friend the Earl of Gloucester a secret messenger bearing coins and a pair of gilded spurs, he at once grasped their significance. A smith was called at night to fix shoes back to front on three horses, to mislead anyone who should track them through the snow. With two companions Bruce made his getaway, and, sparing neither themselves nor their horses, in seven days reached Lochmaben. The suspicion that Comyn had betrayed their secret agreement was confirmed when a courier carrying letters from Sir John to King Edward fell into Bruce's hands.[1] On 10 February 1306 he met Comyn in the church of Greyfriars, Dumfries, charged him with treachery and left him mortally wounded. 'Doubting' that he had killed him, his followers, Lindsay and Kirkpatrick, 'made sure'.

Seven months after the execution of Wallace, Robert Bruce, Earl of Carrick, claimed the throne of Scotland and at Scone on 25 March 1306 was crowned king, Robert I. The young Earl of Fife, whose hereditary right it was to crown the kings of Scotland, was in English custody. His sister Isabella, Countess of Buchan and a Comyn by marriage, nevertheless made a secret dash to Scone to assert the family privilege.

When reports of these affairs reached Edward his fury was again unleashed. Three of the Bruce brothers were separately captured and brutally executed. Their sister Mary and the Countess of Buchan were confined for years in specially built iron and wooden cages, to hang from the walls of Berwick and Roxburgh Castles, attended by hostile English women and allowed privacy only for natural functions. Robert's daughter Marjorie too was subjected to this punishment, but the King later relented and confined the child first to the Tower and then in a nunnery. Bruce's wife, Elizabeth, daughter of Edward's friend, Richard de Burgh, Earl of Ulster, was placed under house arrest in England and under less harsh conditions.[2]

Edward now directed all his energies to the capture of Bruce and any who supported him. Forced into the life of a hunted fugitive, Robert knew well what fate would be his, and his wanderings are well known. Not entirely friendless, in 1307 he gained a foothold on Scottish soil and a small following that included some of Wallace's closest lieutenants. Edward was seriously ill, but as the old warrior prepared for a new offensive, the prospect of battle revived his spirit. On the way to Scotland he was again struck down with dysentery and could travel only a mile a day, carried on a litter. Weak and exhausted he reached the hamlet of Burgh-on-Sands, where, on 7 July 1307, at the age of sixty-eight, he died, a few miles from the Scottish border.

Burton, writing of Edward's new policy of leniency towards Scotland in 1304, 'which experience had taught him' continues: 'His ambition was to be an organiser and reformer – in his own way a benefactor to his race – and this passion was the real source of his severities. He saw before him the splendid vision of the British Isles under one scheme of strong orderly central government, blessing all classes of the community; and his fury when thwarted – his rage against the obstinate self-willed barbarians who baffled his wise projects, drove him to cruelty. He had now found that his projects, so far as Scotland was concerned, would thrive better under a milder policy, and with one great exception, he resolved to conciliate those even who had been in arms against him.'[3]

The one exception was William Wallace, a man whom in other circumstances the King might have respected and, as a soldier gladly welcomed to his side. Today, the main reason for Edward's hatred of Wallace is thought to be the ravaging of the northern counties of England in 1297, and on this matter too Burton offers guidance: 'The English chronicles – which are the only contemporary accounts of this affair – are confused, as all accounts of plundering and devastating inroads, whether by friend or foe, must needs be . . . but it must be remembered that the suffering side had the telling of the story; and it was the policy with the English clergy, who were also the historians, to make out that the Scots were sacrilegious as well as cruel, and reserved their special tortures and indignities for Holy men, and women.'[4]

The Prince of Wales, made to promise that he would boil his father's remains and carry the bones in procession until Scotland was finally subdued, had neither stomach nor inclination for the task – a weakness for which he is sometimes despised. Edward's body, most properly carried south, was later interred in Westminster Abbey.

One of the most powerful kings ever to sit on the throne of England, a cultured and enlightened man, fortunate in his marriage to the gracious Eleanor, his reign could have been – as indeed it began – a glorious one. We owe him much; but ambition led to greed and an insatiable lust for power. His incessant wars, besides denuding the country of its young men, left it in as poor a state as his father's extravagances, and the people turned with relief, if little joy, to their less aggressive new king.

In Scotland hope grew bright. Surviving adversity such as few men have known, Robert Bruce increased in kingly stature and took the patriotic path to Bannockburn. Edward III of England, faced with war against Scotland and France, decided the latter to be the greater gain, and on 4 May 1329 put his seal to the Treaty of Northampton, recognising at last King Robert's sovereignty and the independence of Scotland. The battle was won, forty-two years after the death of Alexander III.

Bruce reigned for twenty-three years; before he died on 9 June 1329 at the age of fifty-five, he had been absolved by the Pope for the murder of Comyn, had established orderly rule throughout the kingdom, and secured the succession, first of his small son David, and second in line his grandson Robert, son of his daughter Marjorie and Walter, the 6th High Steward. The rigours of his life had taken their toll and forced Bruce into retirement. Arrangements for governing the realm after his death he entrusted to Sir James Douglas and Thomas Randolph, his own nephew, on whom he bestowed the Earldom of Moray.

The Black Douglas, as James was known, was killed in Spain on his way to the Holy Land, carrying in a silver casket the heart of his king, which Bruce desired to be buried there, since he could not himself fulfil his intention of leading a Crusade.

David II was five years old at his accession, and married to Joan, sister of Edward III of England. At his coronation the following year he became the first King of Scots to be anointed by permission of the Pope. Thomas Randolph, described by Buchanan as 'inferior in bravery and military skill to none of our Scottish kings and in the arts of peace far superior to them all,'[5] was appointed by the Scottish nobility 'with universal approbation' to the office of regent.

Old grievances surfaced again; exiles who had lost their lands under the late king, or whose lifestyle was curtailed by Randolph's stern discipline, were eager for restitution and revenge. A most able governor, the great earl died only three years after Bruce.

Edward Baliol, son of the long-dead John, seized his chance. With the knowledge if not the connivance of the King of England, he assembled an army and a fleet and sailed for Scotland, arriving in the Firth of Forth. Malcontents and others ripe for adventure rallied to him, defeating the loyalists at Kinghorn and Dupplin, and capturing Perth. From there Baliol proceeded to Scone and in August 1332 had himself crowned king by William Sinclair, now Bishop of Dunkeld.

Little King David and his queen were despatched hastily to France, into the care of Philip VI. Sir Andrew Moray, son of Wallace's companion-at-arms, was the third husband of Christina Bruce, and was thereby David's uncle. Appointed regent, he marshalled his forces and struck at Baliol by night, forcing that king to flee in his nightshirt. Once again the hour brought forth the man. In the two years of his regency Sir Andrew covered himself with glory. He died in 1338 at the age of forty, 'universally lamented'.[5]

For the next twenty years Scotland was torn apart by war with England.

Edward invaded France, the Hundred Years War was beginning, and David, no doubt anxious to assert himself – and prodded by Philip – invaded the north of England in 1346. Taken prisoner at Neville's Cross in October and held in the Tower of London for eleven years, his release was procured by a huge ransom his country could ill afford, and at last he came home.

A more terrible invasion meanwhile, in 1349, put aside the urgencies of war. The Black Death, the plague scourging Europe, swept the British Isles, receding and recurring over a twenty-year period, wiping out perhaps a third of the population. By 1355, however, Edward was again in Europe, defending his property of Aquitaine against the French.

David in middle age was without an heir, and in 1363, by an agreement drawn up in London, the Crown of Scotland, at his demise, was to pass to Edward, and Scotland would be freed from further payment of the ransom still outstanding. People still living who remembered Wallace, knew Bruce, had fought in and shared the tremendous struggle, were not prepared to make the sacrifice. As he might have expected, David's subjects rejected the proposition with 'tumultuous clamour'. The vicissitudes of his reign, years of exile in France as a child, his young manhood spent in idle captivity, must be weighed against his incompetence as a ruler. He died in 1371 aged forty-seven, and was succeeded by his nephew Robert, seven years his senior and, ironically, the father of thirteen legitimate children.

This king, Robert II, was cast more in the mould of his grandfather, and fought with distinction in his earlier years. Approaching old age when he came to the throne, his reign and that of his son John, known as Robert III, were undistinguished. So began the Stewart dynasty.

In a field hitherto dominated by English chroniclers, Scottish writers were beginning to make their mark. Wyntoun, Barbour, and others preserved the ancient and recent past; John of Fordun set off on his fact-finding tour of the British Isles, to restore the records and rewrite Scotland's history. A century later Harry was composing his poem, which, not surprisingly, and in contrast to the milder tone of those earlier writers, bristles with a hatred of the English prevalent in Wallace's day.

Bards and scholars flourished in the fifteenth century; universities were thriving, genuine historians like Major and Boece were replacing mere chroniclers, and in James IV the Scots found a strong and popular king. His marriage at the age of thirty-one to Margaret, the fifteen-year-old elder daughter of Henry VII of England brought about a happier relationship between the two nations, all too soon to change with the accession in 1509 of Henry VIII, and the loss of James's life on Flodden Field in 1513.

# Chapter XIII

Elizabeth I of England died on 24 March 1603, after naming as her successor James VI of Scotland, son of the ill-fated Queen Mary and Henry Stuart, Lord Darnley. The union of the two nations into 'one loving people' was a remark James frequently and happily repeated, his peaceable accession an occasion for thankfulness in both kingdoms. There were no riots, no hostile demonstrations on the streets as the Scottish monarch traversed the counties of England, only joyous crowds to proclaim him and a hospitality so lavish that his progress to the capital took a month. At Westminster Abbey on 27 July 1603 came the Union of Crowns when James, seated on King Edward's Chair, the Stone of Destiny beneath, was crowned James I of England, and the prophecy of the Stone was fulfilled. The King promised to visit his native land every third year, but it was in fact fourteen years before he again set foot on Scottish soil, and the visit caused unrest and dissatisfaction. His apparent preference for English society, climate and customs did nothing to enhance his popularity in a country further impoverished by the removal of the court to the south. James died on 23 March 1625, and was succeeded by his son, Charles I. The execution of that monarch in 1649, institution of the Commonwealth and Civil War, occupied the next decade.

During Cromwell's invasion of Scotland the royal regalia were moved to Dunnattor Castle, thought to be impregnable. The Keeper's wife, Mrs Ogilvie, without her husband's knowledge hatched a plot with the minister's wife, Mrs Granger. The latter was to visit the former, which she did as the Cromwellians were besieging the castle. They allowed her to pass, and when she left it was with the regalia concealed about her person, and that of her maid. Under the stone slab floor of his church at Kinneff the minister buried the crown, sceptre, and Sword of Honour – a gift to James IV from the Pope in 1507. The Ogilvies were thrown into prison, the courageous lady dying there, but neither ever revealed the secret. The treasure remained in this most unlikely place for nine years: it was brought to light at the Restoration of Charles II in 1660. An English crown, made especially for him and known as 'St Edward's' is the Coronation Crown we know today.[1]

But it was not until 1 May 1707 that the dream of James and the English sovereigns before him became a reality. England and Scotland became the United Kingdom of Great Britain. On 6 May, in a speech from the throne, 'rendered in a tone of quiet satisfaction,' Queen Anne gave assent to the Act. Under the terms of Union, the Honours of Scotland, as the regalia are known, were to remain there. They were packed away again and gradually forgotten.[2]

By the middle of the eighteenth century the Scottish nation was looking to its past. Through the might of their pens, writers and poets – notably Burns and Scott – had revived and were reviving patriotic spirit – a revival in which the Prince Regent was to play a sympathetic and not insignificant part. Burns greatly admired Wallace and Bruce, immortalising both in the poem *Bruce's Address to His Troops before Bannockburn:*

Scots, wha hae wi' Wallace bled,
Scots, wham Bruce has aften led,
Welcome to your gory bed,
Or to Victorie!

While several private edifices were erected, there was no official monument to Wallace, and the first movement in 1818 attracted little support. The poet Wordsworth, touring the country in 1803, crystallised national sentiment:

. . . I would relate . . .
How Wallace fought for Scotland; left the name
Of Wallace to be found, like a wild flower,
All over his dear Country; left the deeds
Of Wallace, like a family of Ghosts
To people the steep rocks and river banks,
Her natural sanctuaries, with a local soul
Of independence and stern liberty.[3]

Persuaded by the enthusiasm of Walter Scott, the Prince Regent issued a warrant in 1817 for the opening in Edinburgh Castle of a chest thought to contain the regalia, though no one knew for sure where they were. The search proved fruitful, and Scott, who was present, received a knighthood shortly afterwards. Once more the Honours saw the light of day and have remained on display in the castle ever since. Five years later the Prince, now George IV, visited Scotland – the first British sovereign to do so – and the Honours were carried in procession through the streets of the capital. Among the gifts presented to the King was a box made from the oaks of Ellerslie and Torwood that had sheltered Wallace. The King endeared himself further as he spoke of "the good and honourable service done of old by William Wallace for the defence of that our kingdom".[4]

Following King George's timely acknowledgement came the discovery in 1829 of the trading document to the Mayors of Hamburg and Lubeck, the documents in the Tower of London and in the Chapter House, Westminster. From all this flowed renewed interest in the life and career of Wallace, to which the many biographies published in the nineteenth century bear witness. In the upsurge of patriotic fervour the 'Monument' issue surfaced again. This time (1851) the promoters were determined, and through competitions and advertisements funds began to swell. Slowly at first, then in full spate the contributions came, from home and from Scots scattered around the globe. The leading promoter was the Rev. Dr Charles Rogers, and fortunate we are in having his full personal account of these affairs.[5] He favoured Abbey Craig, overlooking the scene of Wallace's great victory, and on 24 June 1856 an inaugural meeting, under Lord Elgin, collateral descendant of Bruce, was held at the proposed site. Trainloads of people in a multitude of tartans, with ancient banners and battle honours added colour and interest. It must have been an impressive sight.

The competition for design produced nearly one hundred entries, some weird, some wonderful and totally unsuitable – though a pyramid received some public support. Still the subject evoked mixed emotions; according to a letter to the Lord Advocate from William Stirling, dated 20 January 1859, there were many who would prefer that Wallace 'remain uncommemorated except in that page of our annals that he has made so bright'. In other quarters there was a feeling of national reproach – a debt unpaid – and for the visiting stranger no focal point, no shrine. Mr Stirling (later a baronet) nevertheless proposed a 'tall and stately tower' and this plan was adopted. Yet another competition for design was won by Glasgow architect, Mr John T. Rochead, for which he was awarded £50.

In 1861 on the same date as before – 24 June – 'crowds not seen on the Plains of Stirling since Bannockburn 1314' assembled at the Craig for the laying of the foundation stone. Thirty regiments of volunteers, by permission of Field Marshal HRH the Duke of Cambridge (grandson of George III), various public bodies, representatives of 200 Masonic lodges, and forty bands, all assembled in King's Park, Stirling, marshalled under General Sir James Maxwell Wallace.[6] The huge procession marched to the Abbey Craig, arriving about 3 o'clock.

The Field Marshal, on behalf of the Army, presented to the meeting the sword of Wallace; Lord Elgin sent the sword of King Robert, and the Duke of Montrose that of his ancestor, Sir John Graham. Massed bands played the air to 'Scots, Wha Hae . . .' and the assembly, swelled by the public to about 80,000, silent for the blessing, broke into cheering as the foundation stone was lowered into position by the Duke of Atholl, Master Mason of Scotland, and a descendant of Wallace's compatriot Andrew de Moray – a point worth noting against the argument of Andrew's seniority over William. At that precise moment the Union Jack was hoisted as a signal, and the military salute of twelve guns from Stirling Castle proclaiming the 'cordial consent' of Queen Victoria. In his speech Dr Rogers said, "Could Wallace have desired other than a Bruce to inaugurate this monument; other to lay the foundation stone than a Murray?" and he tells the charming story of a descendant of Wallace's family in her eightieth year determinedly climbing the 300-foot Craig to put mortar to the stone.

Many stirring speeches were delivered this day, and again at the Monument's completion in 1869. Built of local stone, 220 foot high, massive and strong, it stands where Wallace stood on 11 September 1297 to direct the Battle of Stirling Bridge. A thirteen-foot statue of the patriot in bronze, placed in a niche built to take it on the southern front, was unveiled by the Marquis of Bute on 25 June 1887.

Much has been written and argued about the two-handed sword believed to have belonged to William Wallace. A pronouncement by an expert in 1825 that such a weapon did not exist in the thirteenth century, received wide publicity at the time and is still being put forward. But from the then Secretary of State for War, and from

HRH the commander-in-chief of the Army, came instructions to the major general commanding forces in Northern Britain, through to the officer commanding Stirling Castle, that the Wallace Sword be delivered into the care of Dr Rogers, and through him to the Monument. The ceremony took place on 17 November 1888. Receiving the weapon from Colonel Nightingale, in his speech of reply Dr Rogers said, "You have handed me the Sword of Wallace, and so conferred upon me one of the greatest honours which any Scotsman has received." Dealing briefly with the betrayal of Wallace and the removal of his sword by Sir John Menteith to Dumbarton Castle in 1305, he then gave a convincing report of its authenticity, with information gathered from the accounts of the Lord High Treasurer, dated 8 December 1505:

"... the sum of 20/- (equal to £30 of present money) for binding the Wallas Sword with 'cords of silk' and providing 'ane new hilt and plomet' also with 'a new scabbard and a new belt' ... at the command of James IV. We learn nothing more for three centuries, when in October 1872 I received from the War Office a letter informing me that when the weapon was sent for repair to the Tower, the Duke of Wellington, as Master General of the Ordnance, submitted it for examination to Dr Meyrick, an authority on ancient swords. In estimating the age of the Dumbarton Sword he was guided by the mountings only, and concluded that it was not older than the one in the British Museum, belonging to the reign of Edward IV and connected with the Earldom of Chester. ... If then the Chester Sword belongs to the year 1475, Sir Samuel Meyrick approximated nearly to the date of the mountings of the Wallas Sword, which occurred thirty years later. But in 1505 the Wallas Sword was an old blade, the weapon so materially shattered it seems reasonable to conclude it was decidedly ancient: moreover, that before it was allowed to rest in Dumbarton Armoury it had been subjected to much hard usage. Its being adorned with silk tassels by the King's command leaves us in no doubt as to it being held in special veneration, while in the register it is described as 'Wallas Sword', no qualifying word of doubt being expressed as to its genuineness.

"Apart from the circumstances that by two separate weldings the blade had been shortened, it is otherwise a duplicate of the two-handed blade of Sir Richard de Lundin, used at the Battle of Stirling 1297 and now preserved at Drummond Castle. Consequent upon Meyrick's judgement, pronounced in 1825, the mountings were removed and a common handle of the fifteenth century substituted – so I was informed by a letter from the War Office in 1872.

"Now we have possession of the Sword . . . and we shall retain it as no unimportant addition to the national regalia."

The weapon, its total length five foot four inches, for years encased and displayed in the Monument's Hall of Heroes, hangs now in the Reception Hall. There let it remain, venerated not as an instrument of terror and destruction, but as a symbol of those ideals for which a brave man, in the eloquent words of the Marquess of Bute, "gave his toil, his sufferings, and his life".[7]

A proposal in April 1913 by the Rt. Hon. Charles Scott-Dickson MP that a plaque be placed in Westminster Hall to commemorate the trial of Wallace was not pursued. The matter was raised again in February 1924 by Mr John Robertson MP and this resulted in a brass tablet being set on or near the spot where Wallace stood before the King's Bench. It was provided by the Office of Works from public funds, and unveiled on 31 October 1924.

Queen Elizabeth, II of England, I of Scotland, following her coronation in Westminster Abbey on a very wet 2 June 1953, toured the whole United Kingdom, and by her command the Honours were again borne through the streets of Edinburgh to the High Kirk of St Giles for the Service of Celebration, which the Queen and the Duke of Edinburgh attended. Who among that throng, gazing on those outward symbols of Scotland's nationality, was unaware of a tall approving presence, and of an even longer procession of those who gave their all in its cause? Three years later a memorial plaque of Scottish granite, placed on the outer wall of St Bartholomew's Hospital at Smithfield in London 'by Scots and friends at home and abroad' was unveiled on 8 April 1956 to the

GUARDIAN OF SCOTLAND
TO THE IMMORTAL MEMORY OF
SIR WILLIAM WALLACE

Few men can have had so profound an influence on the character of a nation; few if any in all history have inspired a love and loyalty so enduring. 'A heroic Wallace, quartered on the scaffold' wrote Thomas Carlyle 'cannot hinder that his Scotland become one day, a part of England, but he does hinder that it become, on tyrannous unfair terms a part of it.'[8]

Scotland must and will retain her own identity in equal partnership, and if there is justification for the claim that the terms of Union in 1707 became the pattern for the British Empire, then let Courage and Integrity cross the bridge of nearly seven centuries and secure for a brave man a more exalted place in the annals of British history than he has this far been accorded.

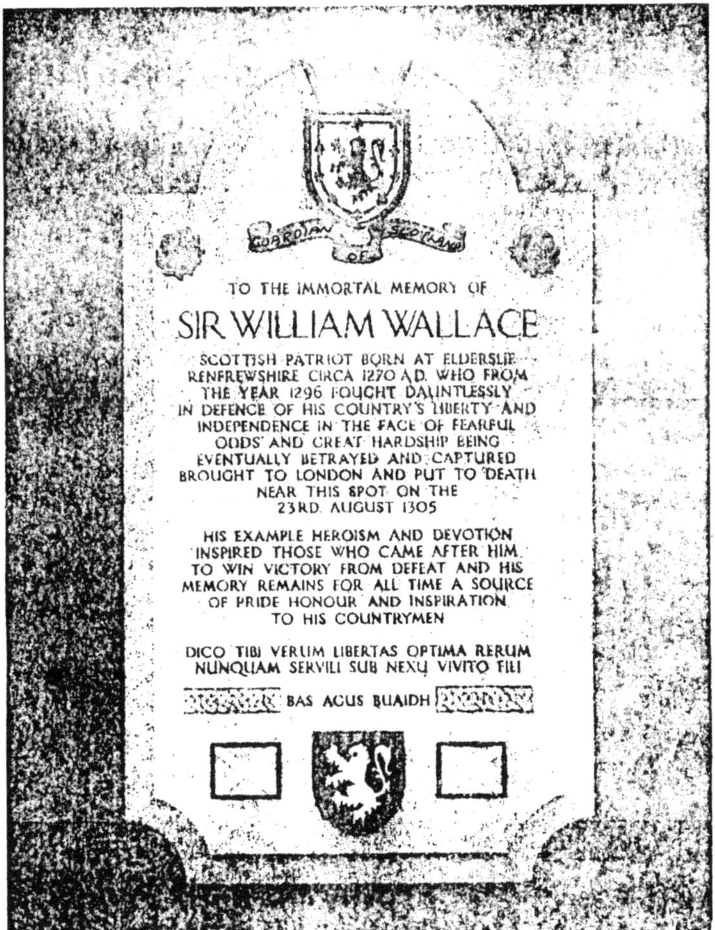

# King George IV's Box

The following is a footnote from p. 310 of *A Historical Account of His Majesty's Visit to Scotland*, published by Oliver and Boyd, Edinburgh, 1822. The author, who is not named, was Robert Mudie.

*'Among the various instances of loyal attachment to His Majesty which deserve to be recorded, there is one which we were in some little danger of overlooking. During the King's residence at Dalkeith-house, a very curious wooden snuff-box was presented to His Majesty by Sir Walter Scott, from the ingenious maker, Mr. Daniel Craig of Helensburgh. The body of the box is made of sycamore tree, with an invisible hinge of the kind at present so much admired, and the lid of it inlaid with authenticated specimens of several varieties of wood, most of which are well known in Scotland, and celebrated in Scottish song. These are so arranged, as to shade and relieve each other by their beautiful diversity of colour. In the centre is a piece of the Cruikston Yew, mentioned in history as the favourite of the unfortunate Queen Mary. Around this are the following:– The Torwood Oak, (of Stirlingshire) whose decayed trunk afforded shelter from his pursuers to the brave Wallace; – the Trysting Tree, near Roxburgh Castle, celebrated in the Border feuds, and mentioned in the novel of Rob Roy; – the Elderslie Yew, which tradition reports to have been planted by Sir William Wallace on his uncle's estate of that name in Renfrewshire; – the Bush aboon Traquair; – Birk of Invermay; – Thorn aboon the Well; – Broom of Cowdenknows; – Alloway Kirk Oak; with all of which the admirers of our Scottish poetry are familiar; – Elm of Waterloo, under which the Duke of Wellington stood during the battle; – the* Victory, *part of the anchor-stock of*

*Lord Nelson's flag-ship of that name. The whole of these are surrounded by a border of Black Oak from the ship* Florida, *which belonged to the Spanish Armada, and wrecked off Tobermory, in the island of Mull, 1588. On the bottom of the box, outside, the words and music of "Auld Langsyne" are painted in a style of uncommon neatness. His Majesty was pleased most graciously to accept this interesting cluster of relics, expressing, at the same time, his admiration, both of the selections of the wood, and of the elegance of the workmanship; and charging Sir Walter Scott with thanks to the ingenious artificer for so acceptable a present.'*

For the above I am indebted to Mr Athol Murray, Assistant Keeper, Scottish Records Office, Edinburgh, and to Mr Antony Shearman, City Librarian, Central Library, Edinburgh.

According to tradition, Wallace's Oak at Elderslie was sixty foot in height, its branches extending forty-five foot north-east, thirty-six foot west and twenty-five foot north.

In the course of his Saturday afternoon rambles* Professor T. C. F. Brotchie met and talked with Elderslie's oldest inhabitant, who as a lad played beneath the oak. He recalled: "It was a michty tree, and there's nane like it hereabouts noo . . . I hae well mind o' the day it was blawn doon – Man, I'll ne'er forget that nicht in February aughteen-fifty-sax [1856].

"The win rummit roon our lum until I thocht the hoose was comin' doon, and it skraighed alang the road there lik' Auld Nick himsel' was fleein' aboot."

'The oak tree that had sheltered Wallace and his men stood on the little green patch adjoining the inn until that February night, a storm which old people recall with feelings akin to horror.'

* Published as a series in the *Glasgow Evening Times* in 1909 and in book form in 1910: *Some Sylvan Scenes near Glasgow* by T. C. F. Brotchie, FSA (Scot.).

# Notes and References

*Frontispiece*
See Murison, p. 158.

*Chapter I*
1 Edith's name was changed to Maud to conciliate the French. Beloved by the English, she passed into history as 'Good Queen Maud'.
2 Burton, vol. ii, p. 41; Murison, p. 30.

*Chapter II*
1 Strickland, vol. ii, p. 131.
2 Buchanan, vol. i, p. 387.
3 Burton, vol. ii, pp. 112–114; McLaren, pp. 55–56.
4 Strickland, vol. ii, p. 134.
5 Edward's own annalist, Rishanger, alone preserves this incident. (See Burton, vol. iii, p. 412.)
6 Buchanan, vol. i, p. 384.
7 Burton, vol. ii, p. 152.
8 Fergusson, p. 6.
9 Buchanan interrupts his progress to expose 'as a shameful retailer of falsehood . . . Richard Grafton, who lately wrote a History of England, that those who read this work may judge what credit is due to this writer. He says, that it is written in the fourteenth book, chap. ii, by Hector Boece, that so much blood was shed on this occasion, that the rivers, which ran through the streets, could have driven a water mill for two days. Now first, Boece has not divided his book into chapters; and next, what Grafton affirms is nowhere to be found in the book at all.' (Buchanan, vol. i, p. 399.)
10 Wyntoun, see *Wallace Papers*.
11 The Ragman Rolls are the parchments containing the terms of homage, together with the seals of the Scottish nobles who vowed allegiance to Edward I in 1296.
12 Henry III, though born at Winchester, preferred to surround himself with foreign 'favourites', many of them his mother's relatives, to whom he gave high office. Simon de Montfort, son of a French baron, claimed the Earldom of Leicester through his grandmother. In 1238 he married Henry's sister, Eleanor, and became a genuinely patriotic Englishman, beloved by the people.

He left England after a quarrel with Henry, but returned to lead the barons in their victory at Lewes on 14 May 1264, which placed in his hands the King and his eldest son, and both were imprisoned. The Mise of Lewes, agreed after the battle, made provision for the King to be guided by a council consisting only of Englishmen. Disagreements over its construction caused de Montfort to devise an entirely new system of parliament, with lords and commons represented. He was killed at the Battle of Evesham on 4 August 1265 by forces under the Lord Edward, and his body and that of his son were foully mutilated.

*Chapter III*

1 Buchanan, vol. i, p. 213–214.

2 Hemingburgh, or Hemingford – to the confusion of the researcher – is known thirdly as Walter of Guisborough, all from his connections in Yorkshire.

3 Almost all that is known of Blind Harry we owe to the historian John Major (1469–1549), who writes: 'Henry, who was blind from birth, at the time of my infancy composed a whole book of William Wallace, and committed to writing in the vernacular, in which he was skilled, deeds commonly ascribed to Wallace. (For my own part, I give only partial credit to such writings of this description.) By the recitation of these however, in the presence of men of the highest rank, he procured, as he indeed deserved, food and raiment.' (See Paterson, p. 19; Moir, p. viii; Fergusson, ref. ed., 1948, p. 118.) Harry's poem, 11,861 lines, believed to have been composed between 1470 and 1473, was committed to MS in 1488. There is some scepticism about Blair's *Latin Buik* as there is now no evidence that it ever existed. But Moir and Paterson name authors who 'speak as if they had seen it' and say that it differed from Harry's in some respects. Moir suggests that the Minstrel may have been a sort of mendicant friar, attached to some religious house where he received education and could engage a scribe. Burton (vol. ii, p. 183): 'he belonged to the days when his craft might be that of a gentleman'.

The MS of 1488, penned by a dean, John Ramsay, who does not name the author, is in the Advocate's Library, Edinburgh. Besides Major's statement, two other factors stand against the argument for Ramsay as the real author: the monarch of the day was sympathetic to the subject, and Harry was still living. It seems rather to have been in his declining years that he recited his poems 'in the halls of the opulent' (Rogers), receiving pensions from James IV. Recorded in the Royal Treasurer's Accounts, the last payment – of eighteen shillings – was made in 1492, probably the year of his death. Dunbar's *Lament for the Markaris*, published in 1508, lists him among 'deceased bards' (Moir's Intro.). His mammoth work is still available to us in the editions, among others, of Dr. Jamieson, 1820 and 1869, and Dr. Moir's, 1889, produced especially, he says, 'for all unacquainted with the ancient tongue'. The poem is wonderfully descriptive, lacking nothing in gory detail. Some of the passages are very moving, some quite beautiful. The Minstrel himself makes no allusion to any affliction, and, complaining only of his lack of eloquence and learning, leaves his reader unconvinced that he was from birth totally blind.

The first complete *printed* edition (1570), of which only one copy exists, said to have belonged to Elizabeth I, is in the British Museum.

4 Stevenson, *Papers*, Intro., xiii.
5 Burton, vol. iii, p. 413.
6 Fergusson, pp. 2–3.
7 From this man would spring the Stewart dynasty. The French spelling 'Stuart' came into general use after James VI succeeded Elizabeth I as James I of England. (As eldest son of the reigning sovereign, Prince Charles is styled Duke of Rothesay, Earl of Carrick and Baron Renfrew, Lord of the Isles and Great Steward of Scotland.)
8 Bute, pp. 21, 44–45.
9 Sir Brian Fitz Alan was Captain of Dundee from 18 June 1291 to 18 November 1292, and at the same time castellan of Forfar (from 4 August) of Roxburgh and Jedburgh; on 13 June he was appointed one of the Guardians and by 23 August was one of the three Justices. With his hands so full of official business 'it has accordingly been suggested that Selby might have been his Deputy'. Murison, pp. 50–51.
10 Rogers, vol. ii, p. 58.
11 An effigy or head of Wallace had previously occupied a niche in the wall of the old prison house, pulled down to make way for a new building. The proprietor, Mr Henry Cowan, a merchant, 'patriotically erected a statue to replace the one destroyed. Whether the head of the present effigy is a copy of the former

one, we cannot say, but that such a relic existed there at all seems in so far to countenance the statement of Blind Harry.' (Paterson, p. 43, note.) Rogers, vol. ii, Monuments to Wallace, gives the date of Cowan's statue, 1809.

12 This is taken to be Thomas the Rhymer of Erceldoune, who foretold the death of Alexander III, and the Battles of Falkirk and Bannockburn. He is believed to have spent his last years in retirement at the Priory of Faile, and to have died about 1297. His real name was Thomas Learmonth.

13 This Sir Henry de Percy became the first Lord Percy on being summoned to parliament by Edward I in 1297. He obtained in 1309, from Antony Bek, Bishop of Durham, by purchase a grant of the Barony of Alnwick, in Northumberland. (Burke's Extinct Peerages. 1831.)

Lord Percy fought against King Robert Bruce at Bannockburn in 1314, and died the following year, succeeded by his eldest son.

14 Murison, p. 57.

15 Murison, p. 51.

16 Moir, notes, bk. 1, p. 145.

17 Murison, p. 33.

18 Buchanan, vol. i, p. 401.

*Chapter IV*

1 Paterson, pp. 54–55.

2 Rogers, vol. i, p.100.

3 Some other relationships given by Harry often called into doubt need not be so far-fetched as they at first appear. Infant mortality and the death-rate of women in childbirth made the begetting of heirs an almost desperate priority. Marriages were arranged from the cradle, hopefully to perpetuate or to establish a desirable lineage. A middle-aged widower did not choose a second or third wife his own age; rather would he select a maiden with all her child-bearing years before her. Thus, grandsons and sons were contemporaries. The nephews of Wallace could quite comfortably be older than he – indeed, Halliday's eldest daughter is said to be the wife of Sir John Graham; she need not have been his age. 'Young Auchinlek' Harry married to the widow of the elderly Sheriff of Ayr (making that youth the uncle-in-law of Wallace), and the marriage 'has issue'. There is nothing incredible here, except that this relationship would not have been

established before June 1297, as will be seen.
4 Rogers, vol. ii, p. 22.
5 Paterson, N. p. 94.
6 See Baillie, *Dictionary of National Biography*.
7 Murison, p. 54.
8 Lingard, vol. ii, p. 534, N.

*Chapter V*

1 Murison gives Wallace's age here as sixteen (p. 69) This must be a mistake. On p. 45 he accepts the date of birth as 1274–1275, and referring to the flight to Kilspindie (p. 49) says 'preferably 1291, when Wallace was in his seventeenth year.'
2 Harry's heroes would of course destroy their enemies. A Sir John de Graystock who fought for Edward in Scotland, and is believed to have died without issue in 1305, may well be the baron referred to.
3 Murison, p. 62.
4 Wyntoun, see *Papers*.
5 Wyntoun, see *Papers*.
6 The *Scalacronica* of Sir Thomas Gray.
7 Burton, vol. ii, p. 184.
8 Burton, vol. ii, p. 115.
9 Buchanan, vol. i, p. 401.
10 Fordun.

*Chapter VI*

1 The *Cottonian* and the *Harleian* Manuscripts. Both are in the British Museum.
2 Bute.
3 Murison, p. 74.
4 'Malcolm III (1057–1093) wishing to cross the River Spey, found assembled on the opposite bank a much more numerous army than it was thought possible the country could produce, ready to dispute the passage. The standard-bearer hesitating, Malcolm snatched the ensign from him and gave it to Alexander of Carron, a knight remarkable for courage, whose posterity always from that time enjoyed the honour of carrying the royal standard in war. He afterwards had the name Scrimiger [Scrymgeour] substituted for Carron, on account of having overcome, by valour alone, an eminent master in the art of fencing who boasted greatly

of his skill, while he was almost ignorant of the science.' (Buchanan, vol. i, p. 343.)

5 Buchanan, vol. i, p. 403.

6 Moir, notes, bk.6, p. 410.

7 See Paterson's Append. The Kerlies of Cruggleton, pp. 360–361. From Captain Denniston's *Legends of Galloway*, 1825: 'Kerlie, the friend and staunch supporter of Wallace, is stated to have been in possession of Cruggleton before the war of independence broke out. Tradition says so, and Captain Denniston supports it, on the authority of Father Stewart. He quotes – "In the year 1282 Lord Soulis came on a friendly visit to Cruggleton, and finding the place but weakly garrisoned, he introduced a number of his followers, sufficient to overpower it, and expelling the chief of the Kerlies, he held the castle for the King of England, whose vassal at that time he was."

'Kerlie is said to have made a number of ineffectual attempts to dislodge the powerful intruder, in which his remaining followers were either slain or dispersed, and that he, with true patriotic zeal, at length joined Wallace at the battle of Loudoun Hill, 1296.'

(The date 1282 is questionable; England and Scotland had no serious quarrel then. Would Alexander III, jealously guarding his kingdom, have allowed the appropriation of so strong a fortress by an English lord?)

8 A court of justices travelling on a circuit.

9 Mackenzie, bk. 4, lines 32–38.

10 Archbishop from 1292 to 1313.

11 Hemingburgh's figures later historians consider exaggerated, while allowing that the Scots were heavily outnumbered. The population of Scotland in the thirteenth century was about half a million; of England three to four million. Hemingburgh alone is responsible for the stories of Lundin's behaviour.

12 Rogers, vol. ii, mentions descendants of 'Jhon the Wricht', nicknamed 'Pyn'.

13 There is a later incident of a cut bridge over the Tay.

14 Fergusson, p. 43.

*Chapter VII*

1 Moir, notes, bk. 7, p. 1214.*

2 The Minstrel does not subscribe to Sir Richard Lundin's defection; he names him a consistent supporter of Wallace and the patriotic

cause. (He is said to be the lineal descendant of a natural son of William the Lion. Paterson, p. 141.)

3 He was eventually sent to Bailleul, his estate in France, where he died in 1315, the year after Bannockburn.

4 *The Scottish Chiefs* by Miss Jane Porter, 1841, pp. 365–397.

5 Buchanan, vol. i, p. 403.

6 It was this Sir Andrew de Moray, posthumously born son of Wallace's compatriot, who in 1326 became the third husband of Christina Bruce. Appointed Regent in 1332 for the ten-year-old David II, son of King Robert the Bruce (I), he died in 1338. See genealogy.

7 Murison, p. 90.

8 Paterson, N. p. 179.

9 Buchanan, vol. i.

10 Ibid., p. 404–405.

11 Paterson p. 198; Murison p. 99.

*Chapter VIII*

1 Murison, p. 108.

2 See *The Scottish War of Independence* by E. M. Barron, 1934.

3 Moir, notes, bk. 10, p. 205.

4 Porter, N, pp. 348–349; Fergusson, p. 89.

5 Hume, pp. 428–430.

6 Hailes, see Murison, p. 105.

7 A descendant of Wallace's family, General Sir John Alexander Wallace 'enjoyed the special confidence of the Duke of Wellington'. One of the great soldiers of his day, the General died on 10 February 1857 aged 82. See Rogers, vol. i; genealogy table, Craigie; also *The Great Duke* by Sir Arthur Bryant, 1971.

8 Fergusson, p. 83.

*Chapter IX*

1 *The Fair Maid of Perth* by Sir Walter Scott, 1877, pp. 86–89. Murison, pp. 111–113.

2 Blind Harry's *Wallace* (1570) and Moir's Intro.

3 Murison, p. 126.

4 Murison, p. 114.

5 Stevenson, *Papers,* Doc. No. xvii.

6 All Saints' Day, 1 November. See Rogers, vol. ii, for a facsimile of this and the charter to Scrymgeour. Murison, p. 114.

7 Paterson, N, p. 277.
8 Stevenson, Intro.

*Chapter X*
1 Murison, p. 117.
2 Murison, p. 128.
3 Murison, p. 137; Fergusson, p. 108; Paterson, p. 295.
4 Buchanan, vol. i, p. 410 and N.
5 Murison, p. 134; Lingard, p. 571.
6 Murison, p. 140.
7 Fergusson, pp. 114–115.
8 Buchanan, vol. i, p. 412.
9 Fergusson, p. 124.
10 Burton, vol. ii, p. 229.
11 Stevenson, p. iii.
12 Daughter of Philip III of France, half-sister of Philip IV.
13 Buchanan, vol. i, pp. 427–428; Paterson, N, pp. 304–305.

*Chapter XI*
1 Fergusson, p. 5.
2 Murison, pp.152–153.
3 One story persists to this day respecting the appearance and prowess of Wallace and Bruce. It originated in the works of the sixteenth-century historian Hector Boece, and it is recounted by Miss Porter in *The Scottish Chiefs*, Append., 1841. 'About the latter end of the year 1430, King James I (Scotland) on returning to Perth from St Andrews, found his curiosity excited to visit a very old lady of the house of Erskine, who resided in the castle of Kinnoul. In consequence of her extreme old age she had lost her sight, but all her other senses were entire, and her body yet firm and active. She had seen William Wallace and Robert Bruce in her earliest youth, and frequently told particulars of them. The King, who entertained a love and veneration for great men, resolved to visit the old lady, that he might hear her describe the two heroes. He therefore sent a message acquainting her that he would come to see her the next day. When she was told that the King was approaching, she went down into the hall of her castle, attended by a train of matrons, many of whom were her own descendants. She advanced to meet his Majesty so easily and gracefully that he doubted her being blind!

'At his desire she embraced and kissed him. He took her hand, and made her sit down on the seat next him, and then, in a long conference, he interrogated her on ancient matters. Among others, he asked her to tell him what sort of man William Wallace was; what his personal figure, what his bearing; and with what degree of strength was he endowed. He put the same comparing questions to her concerning Robert Bruce. "Robert" said she, "was a man beautiful, and of fine appearance. His strength was so great that he could easily have overcome any mortal man of his time, save one! Sir William Wallace! But in so far as he excelled other man, he was excelled by Wallace, both in stature and bodily strength! For in wrestling, Wallace could have overthrown two such men as Robert. And he was comely, as well as strong; and full of the beauty of wisdom.' (Wallace died in 1305; Bruce 1329; a remarkable lady indeed!)

Paterson remarks, n. p. 54, 'No great reliance is to be placed on the statement of Boece, still it is probably no unfair statement of the powers of the two warriors.'

4 Paterson, xxx; Porter, Append., p. 555.
5 Burton, vol. ii, p. 181.
6 and
7 Major, see Murison, pp. 95, 156–157.
8 Stevenson, *Papers.*
9 Murison, p. 46.
10 Ellerslie remained in the possession of the Wallace family until 1769. Wallace House, on the site of the original, for years shored up with timbers, has in recent times – and not without controversy – been demolished to its foundations, allowing the formerly incongruous monument nearby to come into its own.

*Chapter XII*

1 James Aikman, Buchanan's translator, in a note, vol. i, p. 411, says, 'Lord Hailes *doubts* the generally received account of the origin of the revolution which gave Scotland liberty, apparently because it must rest upon the testimony of Scottish historians. His Lordship, in his rigorous examination of their evidence, has certainly found some minor circumstances unaccounted for, but the leading and only important facts, as stated by Buchanan, remain *doubted* indeed, but uninvalidated, and no other or better authenticated have been substituted.' Buchanan, see index.

2 Mackenzie, notes, bk. 4, p. 55.*
3 Burton, vol. ii, pp. 223–224.
4 Burton, vol. ii, p. 195.
5 Buchanan, vol. ii, p. 25.

*Chapter XIII*
1 Burton, vol. vii, pp. 142.
2 Burton, vol. viii, pp. 139, 197.
3 From William Wordsworth's *The Prelude*, composed between 1799 and 1805.
4 Rogers, vol. ii, Monuments.
5 Rogers, vol. ii, Monuments, and Traditions.
6 Sir James, b. 21 Feb. 1783, d. 3 Feb. 1867, commanded troops at Birmingham during the Reform Bill agitations (1831) 'with a good-humoured speech gained the ear of the mob, who dispersed peacefully'. See genealogy.
7 Bute, see Rogers, Monuments.
8 Carlyle, p. 11.

* *Calendar of Documents Relating to Scotland*, edited by Joseph Bain, 1884
Vol. ii, No. 1178 (Moray's son).
Vol. ii, No. 1851 ('kages').
Vol. ii, No. 1910 (Marjorie Bruce).
Vol. iii, No. 48 (Countess of Carrick) (the Queen).
Vol. iii, Nos. 227, 340 (Marie Bruce).

# Bibliography

In order of publication:
Henry the Minstrel (Blind Harry): Poem, *Schir William Wallace*, 1st printed edition 1570. British Museum.
Buchanan, George: *History of Scotland*, 4 vols. Vol. i, translated Aikman. Blackie, Fullarton & Co., Glasgow, Edinburgh, 1827.
Stevenson, Joseph (editor): *Documents Illustrative of the Life and Times of Sir William Wallace* (*Wallace Papers*). Maitland Club, 1841.
Porter, Jane: Novel, *The Scottish Chiefs*, notes and appendices. Frederick Warne & Co., 1841.
Carlyle, Thomas: *Past and Present.* Chapman & Hall, London, 1843.
Strickland, Agnes: *Lives of the Queens of England*, 12 vols. Vol. ii. Henry Colburn, London, 1844.
Paterson, James: *Wallace, the Hero of Scotland.* William P. Nimmo, 1865.
Bute, John, Marquess of, Kt: *The Early Days of Sir William Wallace.* Alex. Gardner, Paisley, 1876.
Rogers, Rev. Charles, DD, LLD: *The Book of Wallace*, 2 vols. Grampian Club, 1899.
Moir, James, MA (editor): *Schir William Wallace.* Scottish Text Society, 1889.
Hume, David: *The History of England*, 3 vols. Vol. i. Reprint of 1786 edition. George Routledge & Sons Ltd., 1894.
Burton, John Hill: *The History of Scotland*, 8 vols. Vols. ii, iii, vii, viii. William Blackwood & Sons, Edinburgh, 1897.
*Traditions Respecting Sir William Wallace*, a binding of 6d. editions. Mitchell Library, Glasgow.
Murison, A. F.: *Sir William Wallace.* Scottish Text Society, 1898.
Lingard, John, DD: *The History of England*, 10 vols. Vol. ii. John Grant, Edinburgh, 1902.
Gardiner, Samuel R., DCL, LLD: *A Student's History of England*, 3 vols. Vol. i. Longmans, Green & Co., 1902.
Mackenzie, W. M. (editor): Poem, *The Bruce* by John Barbour. Adam & Charles Black, 1909.
Brotchie, T. C. F., FSA (Scot.): *Some Sylvan Scenes near Glasgow.* Glasgow Evening Times, 1910.
Fergusson, James: *William Wallace, Guardian of Scotland*, revised edition, Eneas Mackay, Stirling, 1948.
McLaren, Moray: *If Freedom Fail.* Secker & Warburg, 1964.

# Index

## GENEALOGY OF SIR WILLIAM WALLACE

Richard Walense or Waleys of Riccarton
First indentified ancestor and founder of the name, 1173, witnessed charters of Walter, 1st High Steward, in reign of David I

| Richard

| Henry

| Adam
Styled 4th of Riccarton, flourished in reign of Alexander II, and 3rd and 4th Stewards

Sir Ranald Craufurd
Early in 13th century created hereditary Sheriff of Ayr
m
Margaret
Heiress of Loudoun

| Sir Hugh

| Sir Hugh

Children of Adam:

- Sir Richard Wallace m Helen Bruce of Carrick
- Sir Malcolm Wallace
'Got the five pound lands of Ellerslie'.
Slain in conflict with English at Loudoun Hill
m Margaret Craufurd

Children of Sir Hugh:

- Margaret Craufurd
- Sir Reginald Craufurd
Sheriff of Ayr.
Hanged at Barns of Ayr, 18 June 1297
m ?*

*(*Harry marries the widow of 'young Auchinlek')*

Children of Sir Richard Wallace and Helen Bruce:

- Adam Wallace
Loyal supporter of his cousin, and later of Bruce
| *(continued next page)*
- Sir Duncan
of Sundrum (Harry names two brothers, Symon and Richard, the latter mentioned at the battle of Blackearnside)

Children of Sir Malcolm Wallace and Margaret Craufurd:

- Sir Malcolm
Quarrelled at Peebles with Sir David Graham, 1299.
'Killed by the English'
- **WILLIAM**
**b. 1270–1274**
**Guardian of Scotland, 1297—1298.**
**Executed at Smithfield, London, 23 August 1305**
- Sir John
Executed in London, 1307

Children of Sir Reginald Craufurd:

- Sir Reginald
Hanged at Carlisle, 17 February 1307
- William
Loyal supporter of his cousin.
'Supposed to be ancestor of Crawfords of Haining in Stirlingshire, and Crawfords in Linlithgowshire'
- ?

Sir John Wallace m Margaret Lindsay of Craigie, their descendants to be known as 'of Craigie', he quitting 'of Riccarton', she her name

Adam Wallace of Craigie

Sir Thomas Wallace of Craigie, b. 1702

Thomas d. without issue, aged 27

Frances Anna† b. 1730 d. 1815 m John Dunlop of that Ilk, 1748 d. 1785

7 sons and 6 daughters

The male representation continued by Thomas, the second and eldest surviving son. He assumed the title of his maternal grandfather and styled himself Sir Thomas Dunlop Wallace*, Baronet of Craigie, m Eglantine Maxwell, 1772, a literary lady of some note.

General Sir John Alexander Agnew Wallace 'Most distinguished soldier, enjoyed special confidence of Duke of Wellington', d.1857 m Janet Rodger, 1829 d. 1862

Ellerslie and Auchinbothie inherited by a younger branch of the Wallaces of Craigie

In the 18th century, John Wallace of Elderslie having no male issue, his younger brother . . .

Cairnhill

. . . Thomas Wallace of Cairnhill became representative of both houses, d. 1748

John Wallace of Kelly
8 sons and six daughters

d.1803 5th son

Grace, nee Stein (her 2nd marriage, 1836) m General Sir James Maxwell Wallace d. 3 February 1867

*Sir Thomas is believed to be the maternal grandfather of the illegitimate Richard Jackson, later Sir Richard Wallace, whose widow in 1879 bequeathed to the nation The Wallace Collection, the largest private collection in the world.*

*The present Chief of the Name is descended from this line.*

*†Mrs Frances Dunlop, the unifying figure. Illustration by kind permission of HMSO.*

## ROYAL HOUSE OF SCOTLAND

## LINE OF SUCCESSION FROM NORMAN TO PLANTAGENET

WILLIAM I The Conqueror 1066—1087 m. Matilda of Flanders

Robert Duke of Normandy

Richard d.1075

WILLIAM II Rufus 1087—1100

HENRY I 1100—1135 m. Edith of Scotland

Adela m Stephen of Blois

STEPHEN 1135—1154

(1) Emperor Henry V of Germany m. Matilda The Empress m. (2) Geoffrey Count of Anjou (His habit of planting a genista in his hat gave to his family the name PLANTAGENET)

HENRY II, 1154—1189 m. Eleanor of Aquitaine

Henry d. 1183

RICHARD I 1189—1199

JOHN 1199—1218 m. Isabella of Angoulême

HENRY III 1216—1272 m. Eleanor of Provence

Richard Earl of Cornwall

Joan

Eleanor m. Simon de Montfort Earl of Leicester

(1) Eleanor of Castile d. 1290 aged 46 m. EDWARD I b. 1239 1272—1307 m. (2) Margaret of France d.1317 aged 36

Edmund Crouchback Earl of Lancaster

Margaret m. ALEXANDER III 1249—1286

John Henry Both died young

Alphonso, Heir to throne d. aged 11

EDWARD II b.1284 1307—1327 Deposed and murdered in Berkeley Castle m. Isabella, Half-sister of Philip IV of France

EDWARD III 1327—1377

Joan m. DAVID II of Scotland

## LINE OF SUCCESSION FROM SAXON TO STEWART

(2) CANUTE m. (2) Emma m. ETHELRED II The Unready m. (1) Elfleda

*Saxon Line restored*

EDMUND II 1016 Ironside

EDWARD The Confessor 1042—1066 succeeded by HAROLD II Killed at Hastings

EDWARD ATHELING

EDGAR The Atheling

St Margaret m. MALCOLM III 1058—1093

EDGAR 1097—1107

ALEXANDER I 1107—1124

DAVID I 1124—1153 m. Cousin Matilda dau. of Earl of Huntingdon; held earldom from 1108

Edith Wife of Henry I of England (Good Queen Maud)

Henry, Earl of Huntingdon d. 1153

MALCOLM IV 1153—1165

WILLIAM THE LION 1165—1214

DAVID Earl of Huntingdon m. Matilda Dau. of Earl of Chester

Allan of Galloway m. Margaret

Isabella m. Robert Bruce 4th Lord of Annandale

Ada m. *Henry Hastings

(1) Joan Dau. of King John of England m. ALEXANDER II 1214—1249 m. (2) Marie de Courcy

Henry

*John

Devorguilla m. John Baliol

ALEXANDER III 1249—1286 m. (1) Margaret m. (2) Joleta (Yolande)

*JOHN BALIOL 1292—1296 m. Isobel, dau. of Earl of Surrey d.1315

Margaret m. *John Comyn The Black Comyn

Alexander 1264—1284 m. Dau. of Count of Flanders

David d. young

Margaret m. ERIC II of Norway

MARGARET The Maid of Norway b. 1283 Queen of Scotland 1286—1290

EDWARD BALIOL Crowned and deposed, 1332

Johanna de Valence m. Sir John Comyn The Red Comyn, murdered by Robert Bruce, 1306

** Claimants for Crown, 1291*

## HOUSE OF BRUCE

Robert de Brus
Came with the Conqueror

Robert Bruce
Accompanied DAVID I to Scotland;.
granted Lordship of Annandale

Robert Bruce
2nd Lord of Annandale

Robert Bruce
3rd Lord of Annandale

Isabella m. Robert Bruce
4th Lord of Annandale

*Robert Bruce m. Isobel de Clare
5th Lord of Annandale
d. 1295

Robert Bruce, m. Marjorie, Countess of Carrick
6th Lord of Annandale,
1st Earl of Carrick
d. 1304

5 sons and 4 daughters

(1) Isobel of Mar m. ROBERT I m. (2) Elizabeth de Burgh
b. 1274
2nd Earl of Carrick
King of Scots, 1306—1329

Isobel
2nd wife of Eric II of Norway
1293

Christina m.
Earl of Mar;
Sir Christopher Seton;
Sir Andrew de Moray
(3 husbands)

Mary
Held in cage at Berwick Castle for 8 years

Marjorie m. Walter Fitz Alan
d. 1316
6th High Steward

DAVID II m. Joan
1329—1371
d. without issue; succeeded by his nephew, Robert Stewart
Dau. of Edward II of England

ROBERT II
1371—1390
1st Stewart king

** Claimant of Crown, 1291*

## GENEALOGY OF ANDREW DE MORAY

Sir Walter de Moravia

Sir William de Moray,
Lord of Bothwell.
d. without issue,
1293; succeeded by
his brother.

Sir Andrew de Moray.
Taken prisoner at
Battle of Dunbar 1296;
held in Tower of
London.

Andrew de Moray.
Captured at Dunbar, imprisoned in England, escaped, returned to Scotland; led uprising in Morayshire 1297; joined Wallace at Battle of Stirling Bridge; was afterwards elected with Wallace General of the army; died of his wounds, November 1297; his son born, 1298.

Sir Andrew de Moray.
In 1326 became 3rd husband of Christina Bruce, sister of Robert I; appointed regent for David II 1332; d. 1338.

## GENEALOGY OF SIR JOHN GRAHAM

Sir David Graham
of Dundaff. Knight
Granted Kincardine by Malise,
5th Earl of Strathern.
d. about 1270.

m

Annabella.
Dau. of 4th Earl of
Strathern

Sir Patrick Graham
of Kincardine.
Swore fealty to Edward I,
1292; present at Baliol's
homage, 1292; summoned to
attend Edward's expedition
to France, 1294;
Killed at Battle of Dunbar,
1296.

Sir David Graham of Kincardine.
Prisoner of English, 1296;
released, 1297, on promise to
attend Edward in foreign wars;
exchanged lands in Cardross with
King Robert for those of old Montrose;
signed letter to Pope, 1320; d. 1324.
Ancestor of 3rd Lord Graham, created
Earl of Montrose by James IV, who
died with him at Flodden, 1513.

Sir John Graham
of Dundaff,
The 'rycht hand'
of Wallace. Killed
at Battle of Falkirk,
1298. His sword
preserved by his
descendants.

Sir David Graham
of Loveth.
Swore fealty to
Edward I, 1292;
captured at Dunbar,
1296; released,
1297, on promise to
attend Edward in
foreign wars;
quarrelled with
Sir Malcolm Wallace
at Peebles, 1299.

## GENEALOGY OF THE PERCY AND WARENNE FAMILIES

SIR HENRY DE PERCY, 9th Feudal LORD OF NORTHUMBERLAND

JOHN DE WARENNE, 6th EARL OF SURREY

William de Percy came with the Conqueror from the village of Percy, near Villedieu.

William de Warenne, came with the Conqueror; created 1st Earl of Surrey by William II (Rufus).

William (2nd Earl)

William (3rd Earl)

(1) William de Blois of Mortaigne, illegitimate son of Stephen, King of England; d. childless. m. Isobel m. (2) Hameline, Plantagenet, illegitimate half-brother of Henry II of England.

Both husbands claimed earldom by right of wife.

William (5th Earl)

John (6th Earl) m. Alecia de Lusignon, 1247, half-sister of Henry III.

b. 1231; a minor when he succeeded; appointed Governor of Scotland by Edward I, March 1296; d. 1304. Succeeded by his grandson.

Sir Henry de Percy d. 1272. Succeeded by his third and only surviving son. m. Alianore, 1268

Isabella m. John Baliol, 1279 Crowned King of Scotland, 17 Nov 1292; deposed, 10 July 1296; d. 1315.

William b. 1256; killed in toumament at Croydon, 1286. m. Joane, dau. of Robert de Vere, Earl of Oxford.

SIR HENRY DE PERCY
Accompanied Edward I to Scotland, 1296; created 1st Baron Percy, 1309; d. 1315.

Edward, crowned King and deposed, 1332.

John, aged 19 when he succeeded his grandfather as 7th Earl; d. 1347 with no legitimate issue.

Alice m. Edmund Fitzalan, 8th Earl of Arundel.